SIX AFTER SIX

IRELAND'S CRICKET WORLD CUP

KEVIN O'BRIEN

with Gerard Siggins

RSA

SUPPORTED BY RSA INSURANCE IRELAND LTD

Published in 2011 by Brickfields Press
69 O'Connell Gardens, Sandymount, Dublin 4, Ireland
brickfieldspress@gmail.com

ISBN 978-0-9569638-0-2

All rights reserved. No part of this publication may be
reproduced, stored in a retrieval system, or in any form or by any means,
without the prior permission in writing of the publisher, nor be
otherwise circulated in any form of binding or cover other than that
in which it is published and without a similar condition including this
condition being imposed on the subsequent publisher.

Book design and production by Elly Design

Printed by GraphyCems Industria Gráfica

© Text copyright Kevin O'Brien and Gerard Siggins

Cover photograph by Getty Images
Other photography © Barry Chambers, Joe Curtis, the O'Brien family,
Getty Images, Rob O'Connor, Paul O'Donohue, Inpho, FX Carty

To Mum and Dad

*for all the support
you gave me growing up*

CONTENTS

1	Warming up	1
2	Taking guard	9
3	Off the mark	19
4	Playing our shots	27
5	Team Ireland	37
6	Winter wonder	47
7	v Bangladesh	55
8	v England	61
9	Aftermath	73
10	v India	81
11	v West Indies	89
12	v South Africa	97
13	v Holland	105
	Afterword	112
	Scorecards	113
	Statistics	120

STAR STRUCK: *Ian Botham walks out to bat at Clontarf in 1990. That's Niall and me, aged six, out in front!*

CHAPTER 1
WARMING UP

I'VE OFTEN SAID THAT I WAS BORN INTO SPORT, BUT THAT doesn't just mean that my family were all sport mad. My mum and dad were actually watching football on the television when I started to make my arrival. Mum had gone to see her doctor on the Friday and he told her not to worry, her sixth child wouldn't arrive until after the weekend. They waited for *Match of the Day* to end before heading into Holles Street hospital in Dublin, where I was born early on Sunday morning, 4th March 1984.

I was down in the club on Park Avenue within a couple of days and have spent half my life down there ever since.

Cricket was just always there in my life as Dad – or Ginger as he is universally known – was a major figure in Leinster cricket for more than 40 years, scoring a record 25,000 runs, and playing 52 times for Ireland. Some of my earliest memories were of being down in Railway with my big brothers and sister. I was only 7 when I was first drafted into the Under 13s when they were short at the last minute – I fielded 20 overs and got the taste for cricket then.

It was a great family to grow up in – not least because we were constantly playing some sort of sport. The games of cricket, hockey and football in the front garden were always 3-versus-3 and we'd mix the teams around. Nialler stood out, and you'd always want him on your cricket team, Paul and Ciara were the best hockey players, while Ger, Conor and Niall were the ones you wanted for soccer.

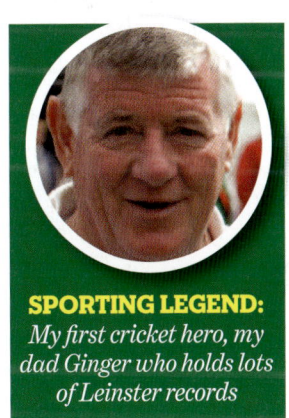

SPORTING LEGEND: *My first cricket hero, my dad Ginger who holds lots of Leinster records*

We held Test matches and World Cups all day long, all year round. And the physical shape of the garden had a huge bearing on the way we still play cricket.

c 1993 **Delighted to collect an early trophy from Leinster Cricket Union president Enda McDermott**

c 1992 **In Scotland with mum and dad we made a stop at St Johnstone FC and Niall and I got to sit in the dug-out**

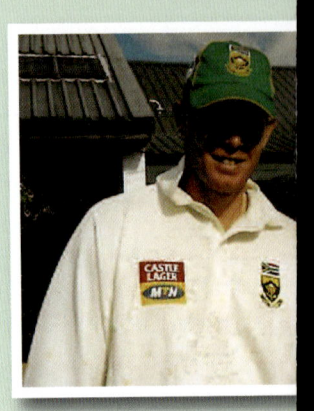

We used the driveway as the wicket, but it didn't run down the middle of the garden so a boundary on the short side counted two and the big side was four. We always bowled towards the house so the big side was on my leg-side, which became the strongest part of my game. Nialler, being left handed, became a strong cutter and driver of the ball, and that still holds today.

Our neighbour on the big side was Dr Rutledge, who had a bush that separated our gardens. Every time we drilled the ball into the bush we had to go in to the house to get a new one, though we would sneak in after dark to recover the lost balls.

1991 First Holy Communion day at Star of the Sea, here I am with Niall

c 1993 The cricket family O'Brien: Paul, mum, dad, Ger, Conor; front: Ciara, Niall and me

July 1998 Two top red-headed seamers – with Shaun Pollock

June 1995 Ted Mullen's neat scorebook shows I was out for 1 to Eoin Morgan!

Conor and Paul are also quite leg-sided players while Ger, who we call Cloughie, was just agricultural.

Nialler always stood out in those garden Tests. He could bat all day while I would always chip it out of the garden once I got to 15 or 20. My eldest brother Paul always got me out. He was a right-arm bowler but when I was batting he'd bowl left-arm slow swingers which I just couldn't hit.

We used a pad for stumps and would play all year round if it was dry. Mum and dad would be going mad inside the house at the constant thumping of the tennis ball against the door and windows, but we never once broke any glass.

The back garden was grass but we very rarely played there. One day myself and Nialler cut and rolled this length in the back garden and tried to prepare a pitch, but as hard as we tried it was too uneven and the ball would end up stopping and rolling along the ground.

Dad was a legend in Dublin, and I regret that I didn't see him play much. He retired from Ireland before I was born. I only played one game alongside him, when I was 14. He worked for the Revenue Commissioners in Sandymount Green, about 200 metres away from our front door. They had a taverners team and one Friday afternoon he came home early and asked me if I wanted a game as they were short. We were playing in Trinity so we headed in together on the Dart. I was chuffed and got a couple of overs to bowl. It is sad that the only time I got to play with him was a little friendly.

Ginger wasn't just a brilliant cricketer who ended up with more than 25,000 senior runs, he was also a gifted footballer and hockey player. He played wing-half for Shelbourne and was on the bench for a European Cup game against Atletico Madrid. When he gave up soccer he took to hockey and won interprovincial caps with Leinster.

> *They didn't play cricket in Marian, but we had some good players – three of us played for Ireland*

It wasn't all play for the O'Briens of course, and I had to head off to Star of the Sea national school at the age of 5. I wasn't too bad a student when I listened, and had some good teachers in Mr McSweeney, Miss Kieran, Mr Molloy and Mr Sweeney.

I liked school – I was in a class with great lads such as Paul Finnegan and Damien O'Hanlon, who are still my best friends. I was games mad of course, and although the only school sports were Gaelic football and hurling, I took to them as well. I joined the local GAA club, Clanna Gael, and also played soccer for Dublin YMCA.

I joined most of the class in Marian College for secondary school, where

BROTHERS IN ARMS:
I followed Nialler to Star of the Sea, Marian College – and the Irish team

my four brothers had preceded me. They didn't play cricket there, but we had some seriously good players – myself, Niall and Roger Whelan played for Ireland and Paul Ryan was a senior player with Clontarf. When I was in first year Nialler went to the headmaster, Paul Meany, and asked him for permission to set up a team. We tried, but kids of that age aren't great at organising things so it never happened. I'm sure we could have won a trophy or two.

I wasn't a bad student, but Science was the one subject I hated. I got 16% in my Junior Cert mocks! I enjoyed Economics but my favourite subject was Art – I still doodle and would love to get back into it at some stage. Maybe it's in the blood as my granny is a brilliant landscape painter.

IRISH DEBUT:
Pleased as punch to be on the first Ireland U13 side ever, in 1997

Our school did the Transition Year programme, and it did me a lot of good. There were great opportunities to learn new skills and sample new activities. We did sailing, rock-climbing, canoeing and orienteering, but one of the most enjoyable things we did was to visit an old people's home in Cabinteely. We went out there every week for six weeks to talk to the residents, who were very interesting people. One day we were heading out there and Drew Murray and I were waiting in Ballsbridge for the Number 7 bus to arrive. When it did we decided to let it pass so we could just chill at the bus-stop for another 15 minutes. Unfortunately, the Dean of fourth year, Dave Kelly, drove up just afterwards and wanted to know why we hadn't got the bus. Dave wasn't a man to mess with, so we made sure we got the next one.

I was quite immature after the Junior Cert but Transition Year settled me down and I hit the books the year after and worked hard in 6th year, to the point where I ended up with a good result.

CELTIC WARRIORS: Conor Mullen in the football shirt next to me at a Railway U11 game

I started studying accountancy in IT Tallaght in September 2002, but at Christmas the following year I realised I would have to miss six or seven weeks of the course to play for Ireland in the Under 19 World Cup and decided to defer for a year. By the time January 2005 came around again I was working in the Russell Court Hotel, which is owned by Railway legend Rangan Arulchelvan, and so I never went back. I went back to Tallaght to start a marketing course that September, but at the start of second year I was picked for the 2007 World Cup squad so I left again.

My cricket was going well, but I knew it was imperative that I get something behind me in case it didn't work out as a career, so after that World Cup I did a course in marketing, advertising and public relations at the Dublin Business School. I really enjoyed that and its something I'd like to get into when I finish playing.

BIG HITTER: *Playing a not-quite-textbook shot in a impromptu test match in Railway*

CHAPTER 2
TAKING GUARD

HAVING SPENT MOST SUMMER AFTERNOONS PLAYING OUTSIDE the boundary rope in Railway, it was inevitable that I would start playing club cricket when I was old enough.

I had sub-fielded for the Under 11s and Under 13s a few times before I was picked as captain for the Under 11 mini cricket tournament out in The Hills, the club in Skerries in the far north of County Dublin. That was a great tournament and we had a pretty good team.

In the semi-final we came up against Merrion, who were to be our main rivals for a couple of years. We ended our ten overs with 80 for 1, and as the rule was that you divided your runs by wickets lost, we were very happy with our net score of 80. However some Merrion mathematical genius had worked out that if you didn't lose any wickets you couldn't have a divisor – so a score of 1 for 0 would beat 80 for one.

So their batters just patted back everything, blocking full tosses and long hops. I was aged just 10 and going mad – "this isn't a rule, you've made it up!" I roared.

Anyway, Merrion's batsmen, Peter Blakeney and Simon Morrissey, had reached 15 for 0 with just one over to bowl. I was given the ball and with two deliveries left Simon chipped it straight back to me and I caught it!

We won that one easily, but had many good battles with Merrion over the years, especially with Ed Joyce's sisters Isobel and Cecilia. In the Under 11 leagues everyone got to bat four overs even if you were out. One day Cecilia got me out three times in one over of leg spin – she never lets me forget that I was bawling as I walked off the field!

We had a great team, though, and I have a bucket of medals at home from those days. Johnny Lyons was our star bowler: teams just couldn't play him. One day he took 10 for 10 off five overs, another day 5 for 5.

In those days our side included Nialler, Roger Whelan, Kenny Carroll and I – who all went on to play for Ireland – plus Conor Mullen (Ireland A) and good senior players like Graham O'Meara. We were coached by Brian Donnelly who has to get huge recognition for what he did for Railway Union and Irish cricket. All the trophies we won were down to Brian who gave up huge amounts of time to coach us and bring us to games. Brian was helped out by David Carroll, Fred Austin, Patrick Dowling and Ted Mullen, who kept the scorebook.

Dad was still playing so didn't really get involved with the team. He used to bring Nialler down to the club for a net but I never went down because I still considered myself as just a bowler. Dad was much more useful as a role model and mentor, but as I was a teenager I wasn't that inclined to listen to him. Thankfully a lot of it sank in subconsciously.

I remember one day watching Dad and Niall opening the batting against Old Belvedere. We had bowled them out for about 160 but they had a bowler called Owen Butler who was the fastest in Ireland at the time. Nialler would have been about 16, and it was Dad's last season in senior. He hit some cracking cover drives off Buttsy and scored the last of his 15 centuries, while Nialler made 40 not out as we beat them by ten wickets.

Brian Donnelly has to get huge recognition for what he did for Railway Union and Irish cricket

I played a lot of club cricket with the second eldest, Ger, who will admit he is a bit of a trundler. I don't think I played too much with Conor, who gave up cricket early, or the eldest, Paul, who is the one I'm probably closest to of all my siblings. It can be intense playing the international stuff with Nialler, while playing social hockey with Paul is a lot more light-hearted. Ciara was a great cricketer too, but specialised in hockey at which she won more than 150 caps for Ireland.

At Under 13 level Phoenix were our great rivals – they had three

RAILWAY UNDER 12S: *Pictured at a final in Malahide.*
Back: Mark Bradley, Greg O'Meara, Ger Foster, Ross Wynne, Richie Byrne, Kevin O'Brien;
Front: Kenny Carroll, Daniel Sinnott, Roger Whelan, Michael Boland, Niall O'Brien

youth internationals in Imran Masood, Gary Black and Paddy Conliffe – though the last two ended up joining Railway years later! I remember one final out in Phoenix when Mark Bradley got 35 to win the game for us.

I was 11 when I first played on the Under 15s as first change bowler. I moved up the order at that age group and scored 40 while putting on a huge stand with Ger Foster, who made 60.

I was starting to be noticed outside the club and was picked on the very first Ireland Under 13 side coached by Matt Dwyer, where I played alongside William Porterfield for the first time, in a four-team tournament in Fettes College in Scotland. Porty made a class fifty against the hosts and I took 3-10.

FLOWER POWER: *Getting ready to bat in a schoolboy match at Castle Avenue*

I played Under 14s for Ireland too but didn't have a good interpro series at Under 15 level and missed out on the Ireland team. Our coach was Brían O'Rourke who wanted me to bat at Number 3, but I didn't think I was that good a batsman and didn't get any runs.

I got back into the Ireland team for the Under 17s tour to play England at Eton College in 2001. We won all three games and I took three wickets in each. Porty and Eoin Morgan got loads of runs for us and it was on that trip that Middlesex took their first look at Moggy. We won the Under 17 European Championships in Denmark, where I got 4-30 against Scotland in the last game.

We won the European Under 19s in Deventer the following year and qualified for the World Cup, which was due to be held in Bangladesh.

Brían and Adi Birrell made me into a batsman on that trip. I went out as an opening bowler and batting No 8, and came back as a batsman at No 4 or 5.

What happened was that one day at training Adi took Brίaner aside and said "we're missing a trick here with Kev. Get Porty to ask Kev would he bat up the order – at No 4."

Porty came up to me and said, "here lad, what about you batting 4?"

I was quite surprised but as I'm laid back about most things I just said "OK".

Porty went back to the coaches and told them that I'd do it, but Adi told me years later that he wasn't sure if I was really up for it.

That tournament was a massive eye-opener for me as a batsman. Back in Railway I was firmly stuck at 8, 9, or 10 in the order and the chance to go in earlier was fantastic. Only Eoin Morgan scored more runs than I did, and I made 70 against Uganda, 51 against Canada and 95 against West Indies. The guy that got me out in that last game, Lendl Simmons, is the nephew of a guy who played a big part in my subsequent career!

U13S V SCOTLAND: *I'm in front row next to Porty. Coaches are Matt Dwyer, Brian Walsh and Michael Quinn*

RANGAN'S RAIDERS 1997: *I'm 2nd left in back row, between Kenny Carroll and Neville Clarke; Rangan is holding the Intermediate A league trophy*

Back in Railway I was playing on the adult sides from age 12 or 13. I played a lot of 4th XI cricket under the captaincy of Rangan, who was a shrewd tactician. Kenny Carroll and Conor Mullen were on the same team and we had a pair of excellent Aussies called Matt Campbell and Matt Browne. We won the Intermediate League one year with 13 wins out of 14.

Rangan had this great tactic of telling a bowler that he'd keep him on if he got another wicket. I was so keen to bowl that I'd make an extra effort – one day down in Mullingar I bowled 15 overs in a row! Nowadays ECB rules won't allow any kid bowl more than four overs on the bounce but they were different times and Rangan knew how to get the best out of me.

I played a bit on the 3rds but only lasted for about a month on the 2nds before I became a regular on the 1st XI.

I made my senior debut aged 16, on 5th June 2000, against Trinity in College Park. They had a good side and hammered us, and we made a poor score of which my contribution was one run, batting at number ten. Ed Joyce was playing for them, and he had already played for Middlesex. He made about 80 and Trinity only needed ten to win when I came on to bowl.

Ed blocked my first couple of balls and Nialler, standing up, shouted "come on Kev!"

Joycey spotted the red hair and asked Niall was I his brother, and he said I was and told him to go easy on me. Fair play to Ed, he patted back the rest of the over.

I was chuffed walking down to fine leg. A maiden to Ed Joyce! I ended up with 3.3-1-6-0, which wasn't a bad start.

Other members of my family were looking out for me too at that stage. My second or third senior game was out in Clontarf, who had a young, lively André Botha as their pro. I got him out with a long hop which he dragged onto his stumps. They were all out for 160 or so, but we were taken apart by André, who took six-for coming down the hill, and an Aussie called Toby Cohen who took four-for at the other end.

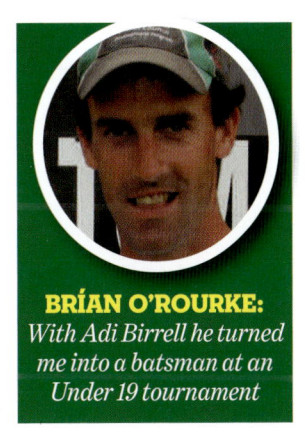

BRÍAN O'ROURKE: With Adi Birrell he turned me into a batsman at an Under 19 tournament

At 120 for 9 I came in last man to join my brother Ger. He nicked one down to third man, but turned down an easy single. Bothsy laid into Ger for protecting me – but if he had got the chance he might have killed me!

In my first full season I played alongside Ger and Niall, as well as Rodney and Greg Molins from the old Carlisle club, and an Aussie called Ian Hewitt. I got about 30 wickets but scored less than 200 runs. Nialler was captain in 2003 before he left to join Kent and he put me up to No 6 where I got a few decent scores.

That was also the summer I had an early taste of the Ireland set-up under new coach Adrian Birrell. I was invited along to Malahide to act as substitute fielder on the final day of a three-day game, and when the game was petering out to a draw Nialler asked Jeremy Bray to fake an injury so I could go on to field for ten overs or so. It was a great experience and one that made me resolve to try my very best to play for Ireland.

The following summer I was off to England myself, this time as an MCC Young Cricketer, which is the nearest professional cricket has to an apprenticeship. It came about because of Philip Hudson, who works with ICC Europe, had spotted me at the Under 17 and Under 19 international tournaments. He recommended me to the MCC coaches Graeme Welch and Clive Radley. Graeme came over to the Under 19 World Cup qualifiers in Holland to check me out in a warm-up game against England. They had hammered everyone else but I bowled the first six overs without conceding a run so I think I impressed him. I ended with 10-6-18-3 and he had a chat with mum and dad about my future.

They offered me a three-week trial and told me to bring over a white shirt, Irish tie, blazer and shoes. Going to matches in a blazer was a new one for me! My first game was against Hampshire at John Paul Getty's ground at Wormsley.

I had two great summers at Lord's, training and playing five days a week in the best cricketing facilities in the world, and working with top coaches such as Radley and Owen Dawkins. MCCYC play in the Second XI Championship, against the other southern 2nd XIs, all of whom take it very seriously. We also got the opportunity to bowl to visiting test teams the day before internationals at Lord's, which was great fun for a teenager. During the test matches we would help out in the MCC shop or help bringing the covers on and off during rain breaks.

I made great friends at Lord's, although there were plenty of Irish guys around at the time too. Porty, Gary Wilson and Gary Kidd were there, and Moggy and Boyd Rankin were with Middlesex. There were a few others I knew too, Freddie Klokker and Daan van Bunge from Holland, Will Gidman who now plays with me in Gloucestershire, and a really good Bangladeshi called Mahmudullah Ryad who is on their test side.

I loved the life in London. Eight or ten of us lived in a youth hostel which

LORD'S DAY: *With MCC Young Cricketers in the famous Harris Garden in May 2005: Ian Young, Nadif Chowdhury, Kevin O'Brien, Andrew Colquohoun, Simon Roberts, Mahmud Ullah Ryad, Kyle Hodnett; Front: Gary Wilson, Shaun O'Brien, John Hughes, Will Gidman*

cost £70 a week for bed and three meals a day. In my second season I took 50 wickets and scored 1,000 runs.

They invited me back for a third year in 2006, and I would have loved to take the chance. But I knew that if I had any chance to make the squad for the 2007 World Cup I would have to go home to Dublin and score plenty of runs. Adi Birrell knew that Porty, Willo and I were playing at Lord's, but he wouldn't have known what sort of standard we were playing at so I returned to Railway.

My first game back was against Cork County, and it was great to see guys who I hadn't played with for two years. I did alright, too, and made 95, caught at long on going for a six. 2006 turned out to be a great season for Railway Union, winning four senior trophies out of the five competitions we entered. It was good to be back.

FIRST SCALP: *Celebrating with TJ after I got Andrew Strauss out with my first ball in ODIs*

CHAPTER 3
OFF THE MARK

MY FIRST TASTE OF THE IRISH SQUAD WAS IN APRIL 2006 WHEN we went to the Eurasia Cup, an 'A' team tournament in Abu Dhabi. Sri Lanka, Pakistan and India sent teams, while we were also joined by fellow associates Holland and UAE. We had a great, young side, coached by Matt Dwyer and captained by William Porterfield. Several of the guys who came into the senior team over the next year were there, including Willo, John Mooney and Roger Whelan. There were some serious cricketers at the tournament, including future stars such as Umar Gul and Mohammed Hafeez of Pakistan, Piyush Chawla of India and Nuwan Kulasekera of Sri Lanka. I had one good knock in that tournament, making 38 against India in a stand of 80 with John Mooney.

I was set to make my debut against England in what was Ireland's historic first ODI on 13th June, but two days before I was called in to the team at the last minute for a Friends Provident Trophy game. Adi used to announce the team the night before games at a team meeting, and that evening he finished with "Kev's 12th man unless Bothsy's out." We were playing Sussex and I was pretty nervous!

The next morning during the warm-up I kept looking over at Andre doing the fitness test.

Mum and dad walked into the Clontarf ground on 11th June 2006, in time to see a photo being taken of me being handed that blue cap with the green shamrock by Roy Torrens. Once they saw that they knew I was the third member of the O'Brien family to play cricket for Ireland.

Sitting in the dressing room I looked round at my team-mates and saw that Adi had stuck a laminated newspaper clipping on the wall over their seats. Each featured one of their greatest successes and was intended to help motivate the guys. I thought about how great it would be to have one of those on my coat hook some day.

My debut match could hardly have got off to a worse start as Dom Joyce and Jeremy Bray were out before we scored a run. Peter Gillespie made 51, but the score was 86 for 5 when I came in. Sussex were one of the strongest sides in England at the time with international cricketers such as Chris Adams, James Kirtley and Mushtaq Ahmed. Kirtley tried to bounce me and I hit him for six. He muttered something about me being just like my brother, so I just told him get up on the roof and collect the ball.

I made 23 and took the wicket of Adams, so I was happy that I was contributing in my first game for Ireland. If I say so myself, I timed my run brilliantly – they didn't have any time to drop me before the World Cup!

The game against England at Stormont was an amazing occasion – it must have been the biggest crowd at a game in Ireland for a hundred years or more. I was quickly into the action, and was happy when TJ threw me the ball. Andrew Strauss was facing, and I bowled him my stock ball – a long hop on leg stump. His eyes lit up and he pulled it straight to André at midwicket!

I discovered afterwards that I was only the third player ever to take a wicket with his first ball in a one-day international.

DEBUT DELIGHT: *Receiving my first cap from manager Roy Torrens as Trent Johnston, Kyle McCallan and coach Adi Birrell look on*

I was busy in the field too, taking three catches, including future team mate Ed Joyce who was making his debut for England.

I took 1-47 and made 35, and did OK at the following European Championships, but Adi must have seen something that he liked, because I was selected in the 15 man World Cup squad at the end of September. The team was picked six months early to allow us to prepare as well as we could – and to allow the guys to negotiate leave from their jobs as postmen, teachers and van drivers.

I had a great year with Railway too, playing every one of the 22 games. Kenny Carroll had an amazing season, scoring 1,000 runs, as did our overseas player John Anderson who also took 40 wickets. I batted No 3, Adrian Murphy No 4, and Conor Mullen only got to bat seven times at No 5. We completely dominated in almost every game.

I made 1,150 in all competitions that year, and scored my first century for the club in the league final against Malahide, which was the first senior trophy we had won for four years. We made 271 for 6, with John Anderson making 80. They had an Aussie pro called Dave Wotherspoon and he made 60 and they got past 100 without loss. I bowled rubbish, 5-0-51-0, but John came on and took 3-15 and they were all out for 160.

It was a great year off the pitch too. I was 22 and most of the guys in the side were around that age, so the partying never stopped. One weekend we made 400 for 3 against Munster, then on twenty20 finals day made 190 against North County and 180 against the Hills. That's 770 runs in 90 overs!

We had the league wrapped up in early August, and then concentrated on the Irish Senior Cup. We beat Limavady in a cracking semi-final but the final against Rush was a real nail-biter. They were a Section A side with top players like Finto McAllister, Brían O'Rourke, Naseer Shoukat, Sadat Gul and Shadid Iqbal, but we were full of confidence – and had Nialler back for the game.

They got 200 and we were cruising at 80-0 off 15, but then we collapsed to 100 for 5. Murph made a brilliant 55 which won us the game. Towards the end it got very nervy, but Roj and Jimmy Rogan were there to finish it off. The Irish Senior Cup is a fantastic competition and very few Dublin clubs have won it, so we celebrated hard that night in Rangan's nightclub Krystle.

BOWLING ON: *A great photo by Joe Curtis of me in action against Gloucestershire in my first season for Ireland*

John Mooney, Kenny, Porty and I went off to Pretoria in October to the ICC's High Performance camp, where we lived and breathed cricket for eight weeks. We worked with top South African coaches such as Kepler Wessels, Eric Simons and Gary Kirsten, as well as England women's coach Mark Lane and the ICC high performance director Richard Done.

Before we went Adi sat us down one by one and told us what he expected of us, what we needed to work on and where we were to be when we got back. The main thing he told me was that if we played any practice matches I was to bat at No 5. I just nodded and said "grand" – I reckoned Adi must have had a plan and his plans were usually pretty good.

We were also over there on a scouting mission, as the other five associates that had qualified for the World Cup would also have four players at the camp. The top associate teams were set to meet in Kenya for the World League, before the World Cup, so Adi wanted us to report back on the strengths and weaknesses of the other players. The four of us used to meet every couple of days to chat about the other players and make notes.

> *'Kev, you're in the team to hit boundaries', TJ said. 'Myself and Adi back you to clear the ropes'*

That didn't seem to do us much good, because our results in the Kenya tournament were awful. We were narrowly beaten in four games, and the only consolation for me was that I finally nailed down my place in the team.

I also discovered my role in a roundabout way. Our first game was against Scotland and I was caught on the deep midwicket boundary for 12. When I got back to the dressing room TJ was padding up and I said "sorry Teej, bad shot".

And he turned and looked at me and said, "Listen Kev, you're in the team to hit boundaries, that's what you're there for. Myself and Adi back you to clear the ropes." That gave me such confidence to express myself, to take chances at the wicket.

BRIAN'S BABES: *Five of Brian Donnelly's old Under 11 team with the Irish Senior Cup we won against Rush in Castle Avenue in 2006: from left: Kenny Carroll, me, Brian, Nialler and Roger Whelan; Conor Mullen is up the front. All of us played for Ireland or Ireland 'A'*

The next game was against Bermuda and Porty and I put on 130 to win; he got a ton, I got 52.

Two days later we played Kenya and that was a real turning point in my inetrantional career. Porty and I set a new Irish record 4th wicket partnership of 227. I scored 142 off 120 balls on a fabulous batting wicket. I've got a ridiculously good record in Kenya – I must average 80 there and about 26 everywhere else!

DING DONG: *I'm pretty delighted here to get the wicket of Ian Bell as Kevin Pietersen turns away*

CHAPTER 4
PLAYING OUR SHOTS

THE 2007 WORLD CUP WAS THE FIRST ONE FOR WHICH IRELAND had ever qualified. We told everybody that we were just going over to try and play well and put Irish cricket on the map – but we knew we had a good chance. The group we were drawn in included Zimbabwe, the weakest of the top sides, and who we had beaten quite easily in 2004; and West Indies and Pakistan who were two of most volatile – they could be brilliant but also awful. We were playing the Windies in their own backyard but it shows how confident we were that we seriously considered we were able to beat them.

Our opening game against Zimbabwe was all swings and roundabout, with a brilliant century by Jeremy Bray, but at the end we had no right to get anything out of it. It was an unbelievable finish.

They needed nine to win when I started the 49th over. It was one of the best of my life – wicket first ball, four dots and then a run out – double wicket maiden!

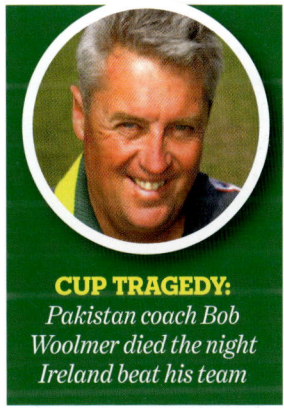

CUP TRAGEDY: *Pakistan coach Bob Woolmer died the night Ireland beat his team*

We scrapped for every ball of Andrew White's last over and a run-out ensured the scores finished level. We knew that in a small group a tie was as good as a win, and we were very upbeat heading into the Pakistan game two days later, on 17th March.

The day before we played Pakistan, Moggy and I had a few drinks in the pool bar at the Pegasus Hotel in Kingston, Jamaica. The Pakistan coach, Bob Woolmer, sat a couple of chairs down and came over for a chat for a couple of minutes. He was delighted for us and said that he thought we had played well against Zimbabwe.

I was there when they pulled the covers off the pitch in Sabina Park on the morning of the Pakistan game, and the track looked very green. Most of the crowd were in by the time we started warming up, and we could see some lads were getting on the beer early. Everyone was wearing green because it was St Patrick's Day – even Pakistan!

TJ won a crucial toss and Dave Langford-Smith bowled a great ball to get rid of Mohammed Hafeez. We took wickets steadily – Shoaib Malik got an edge off one of mine and nicked it to Nialler, but Andre Botha's performance was brilliant. He bowled eight overs, took 2-5, and Pakistan were bowled out for 132 – a better result than we could have dreamed of.

Nialler played the innings of his life. He went in at 15 for 2 and was out at 108 for 5, and he made 72 of the 93 runs scored while he was at the wicket. Everything came off the middle of his bat.

We were 70 for 4 when I went in, and I knew there was loads of time

OVER THE MOONS: *I'll never forget the lap of honour after we beat Pakistan in Sabina Park – here Paul Mooney and I soak up the incredible atmosphere*

THE FAMILY WAY: *Shoaib Malin is out caught N O'Brien, bowled K O'Brien to leave Pakistan rocking on 72 for 6*

left, so I just decided to stay with him. I faced 52 balls for just 15 runs, which is not the way I usually play!

We were in and out a couple of times with rain, but were ahead on Duckworth-Lewis so weren't too unhappy. We needed about 25 when Nialler was out, but then we lost Andy White and Kyle McCallan in consecutive balls. TJ played and missed a few times and I started to wonder whether we could do it at all. I couldn't remember who we had in next, so I asked TJ. When he said "Lanky and Boyd" it didn't make it any better! But then Trent hit the ball into the stand and everything went crazy. It didn't hit me immediately; I was shaking hands with the Pakistanis and the umpires while everyone else was going mad.

When things finally settled down I was grabbed by a TV producer and stuck in front of a camera to talk to commentator Tony Cozier. "Well Kevin," he asked, "what's it like to hit the winning runs?" And I said "I didn't hit the winning runs." Live on TV!

We had a few beers and songs in the dressing room before we hopped on a bus to Ocho Rios, a resort on the north of Jamaica where most of our families and the Irish fans were staying. We had a fantastic night there, and I finally got off to bed at 6am.

I was sharing with Nialler, and he got up early and came back at 11.30am to tell me "Bob Woolmer is dead". I thought it was just a dream, so I went back to sleep and woke again at 4pm when a few of the guys called up to see me. I couldn't believe it, as Bob was a great friend of Irish cricket. The stories that went around afterwards were very upsetting.

That result meant we had qualified for the Super Eights, which meant we had achieved our aim of putting Ireland on the map. After that, everything was a bonus. We enjoyed ourselves, and had every right to.

Everything about that tournament was fantastic. We seemed to spend

JAMAICA RUM: *The team that took on the world in 2007: Andre Botha, Dave Langford-Smith, Niall O'Brien, Eoin Morgan, John Mooney, Boyd Rankin, William Porterfield, Kyle McCallan, Jeremy Bray, Andrew White, Trent Johnston, Adi Birrell, Pete Johnston, Roy Torrens; front: Kenny Carroll, Kevin O'Brien, the local security officers and Matt Dwyer*

a lot of time on Sky Sports, including trying out the famous 'crossbar challenge' – although they didn't even show my effort it was so bad. I would have embarrassed my coaches from my days as a centre-back for YMCA.

I had a couple of good knocks, 48 against Bangladesh (run out) and 49 against New Zealand (also run out). I was told afterwards that the TV

OUT OF AFRICA: *I always seem to get runs against Kenya. This game was in the World Cup qualifiers in South Africa*

commentator in New Zealand blamed Nialler for the second one and said "I wouldn't want to be their mother tonight trying to separate them..." You don't hold grudges though – these things happen in cricket.

My most amazing non-cricket memory from the Caribbean was

visiting the Kaiteur Falls in Guyana, where the water drops 750 feet. I went to Niagara Falls last year and it was tiny compared to it. Kaiteur is deep in the Amazon jungle and we flew there in a tiny six-seater plane. I travelled with Boyd Rankin who was very cramped for space!

Overall we acquitted ourselves well in the Caribbean, and our next taste of the world stage was the ICC World Twenty20 in England, and again we beat one of the "big boys" to qualify for the Super Eights. I got 39 off 17 balls to help beat Bangladesh, when John Mooney and I put on a stand of 50 in four overs. In the Super Eights we had a great chance of beating Sri Lanka after Alex Cusack bowled a brilliant 4-18 off three overs. We only lost by four runs when we should have beaten them, but Twenty20 was quite new to us then.

Our group games had been played in Trent Bridge, Nottingham, which is my favourite ground in the world. And it was there I headed for after our last game at the Oval, as I had signed a contract to play one-day cricket for Nottinghamshire.

They got in touch the previous autumn while I was out in Africa to play some Intercontinental Cup games. I had a stress fracture and couldn't bowl, but batted well in Kenya and scored 171, including 12 sixes. Notts' head coach Mick Newell was obviously impressed because he contacted Phil Simmons and he put us together.

Notts are a very good club with excellent coaches in Paul Johnston and Andy Pick. They had a very strong side too, packed with international players like Graeme Swann, Stuart Broad, Ryan Sidebottom, Chris Read, Samit Patel, David Hussey, Adam Voges, André Adams and Ally Brown. The team was just filled with stars.

I was only there to play Twenty20 and Pro40 games, but it was a good experience for me, learning how to play and train as a professional. The real learning curve was learning how to be a day-in day-out cricketer, which stood to me with Ireland as our programme increased. I'm putting more thought into preparing training schedules and now go in with a plan every time, which I learned from my time at Notts.

That said, I wasn't particularly successful on the field, but got a good 40 in a televised game against Worcestershire and a few wickets here and there. I just didn't do enough to get another contract.

Nottinghamshire were actually my third county – when I was at MCC Porty and I got a game for Durham 2nds, and then in 2008 I went for a trial for Middlesex 2nds – and pulled my hamstring bowling my first over.

All those trips across the water kept me away from Park Avenue, where Railway were having a few ups and downs. In 2007, a very soggy summer in Dublin, we were relegated because we only played three games, but went straight back up in 2008. The following year we won the 45 over league and in 2010, in a memorable day in College Park, won the cup for the first time since 1968. The senior league is the big one for Railway – we haven't won it since 1939. Every other team have won it since we last won it. I hope to play a part in breaking that run someday.

In February 2010 Ireland played the World Twenty20 qualifiers in Dubai, and finished second to a new power on the associate scene, Afghanistan. It was probably best to lose that final, as it meant in the main event we got to play England and West Indies, who at the time were less intimidating than the alternative: Australia and South Africa.

ON TO SUPER EIGHTS AGAIN: *John Boy and I show our delight after we beat Bangladesh at Trent Bridge in 2009*

In the 2010 World Twenty20, again played in the Caribbean, we batted poorly against West Indies, all out for 90, but we bowled and fielded very well against England, keeping them to 120. Unfortunately the game was ruined by the weather and abandoned early in our innings – I'm certain we would have beaten them had the rain kept away for a few minutes more. That was a bit sad, as it would have meant three Super Eights in a row.

Still, we proved again we were gaining more confidence and closing the gap on the big boys: the graph was still sloping upwards.

IRELAND'S 2011 WORLD CUP SQUAD: *Back row: Brendan Connor; Pete Johnston, John Mooney, George Dockrell, Albert van der Merwe, Boyd Rankin, Nigel Jones, Alex Cusack, Gary Wilson, Paul Stirling, Kieran O'Reilly, Phil Simmons; Front: Shirish Buch, Kevin O'Brien, Ed Joyce, Andrew White, William Porterfield, Roy Torrens, Niall O'Brien, Trent Johnston, Andre Botha*

CHAPTER 5
TEAM IRELAND

THE GROUP WE BROUGHT TO THE 2011 WORLD CUP IN THE sub-continent was the best-prepared we have ever had, for any tournament. We had a phenomenal preparation – three weeks in India in November and another couple of weeks in Dubai on the way to the warm-up games. Throwing 20 guys together like that could be tricky, but I can safely say that everyone got on really well with everyone else. Let me introduce you to the boys in green (caps and ODIs are their totals before the World Cup).

WILLIAM PORTERFIELD
Captain, Warwickshire, 113 caps, 44 ODIs

I've known Porty since Under 13s and he's one of my best friends from our time together at MCC Young Cricketers. He's a single-minded player and a class batsman. He went up an extra level when he went to Gloucestershire after the last World Cup. He had a great season for them – and Ireland – in 2010 and was rewarded with a great move to one of the biggest counties, Warwickshire.

Porty's quite a laid back guy and usually just chills out in his room. He likes to relax with a couple of pints, and he could be a bit loose in his younger days in London. He's a huge Man U fan.

PAUL STIRLING
Middlesex, 69 caps, 23 ODIs

Stirlo is a great lad, and a player with a huge future, which he proved again after the World Cup when he made a fantastic century against Pakistan. He's a brilliant pool player and is always happy if there's a pool table in the hotel. Make sure you check out the Cricket Ireland TV channel on YouTube – his ice bath adventure is one of the funniest things you'll ever see. I think he's allergic to water.

ED JOYCE
Sussex, 50 caps (Ireland), 17 ODIs (England)

Joycey's a quiet man, and this trip was the first time I got to know him because he had already gone to England when I was first capped. He's very laid back. When most guys get out they're usually effing and blinding, but Ed just comes in and takes his gear off. He's a very good rugby player – I think he played senior cup in school and, like me and Big Phil, is a Spurs fan. Barry Chambers got an email during the World Cup inviting the three of us to White Hart Lane next season so we're looking forward to that.

NIALL O'BRIEN
Northamptonshire, 107 caps, 40 ODIs

What can I say about Nialler – very little that's printable I suppose! As a big brother he was great, always there for me. He's a brilliant soccer player, and might even have made a career out of it. As it is he is a keen Evertonian and gets to see them as much as possible. He's very big into his music, too, and has a huge collection of sounds.

GARY WILSON
Surrey, 94 caps, 25 ODIs

I know Willo longer and better than anyone apart from Niall and Porty. We came up the Irish youth system alongside each other and played in the U19 World Cup in

Bangladesh. He's a huge Man U fan and you can hear him roaring miles away if they score. He's a keen golfer but I expect that to end when he finally marries the long-suffering Jennifer in October 2011. Porty will be his best man so I can't wait to hear his speech.

ALEX CUSACK (left)
Clontarf, 94 caps, 31 ODIs

ANDRE BOTHA (right)
North County, 139 caps, 40 ODIs

Cusy and Bothsy are the quiet men of the squad – you hardly ever see them. Phil always puts them together so I can't imagine what the conversation is like. They never leave their rooms – every morning on tour there's always one room service tray in the corridor, and you know it's that pair.

Cusy is a big Queensland rugby league fan, and they're both pretty good to have on your side in the touch rugby games. Bothsy called it a day after the World Cup and it was sad not to have such a great cricketer around anymore. He has been a great servant to Irish cricket since he arrived in Clontarf as a teenager and has plenty to contribute still for his new club Terenure.

ANDREW WHITE
Instonians, 187 caps, 49 ODIs

Whitey loves the jokes, but he misses his play-mate Kyle McCallan. But, like all practical jokers, he hates getting pranked himself. It feels like he's been around forever but he's still performing and had a great season in 2010. For a school PE teacher he's not great at rugby – he thinks he's better than he is and he's always at fault when you concede a try. He's a nifty soccer player, but a bit dainty – he'd never put his foot in.

JOHN MOONEY
North County, 99 caps, 29 ODIs

John Boy is passionately patriotic and very proud to play for Ireland. He's an unbelievable sportsman, good at everything he turns his hand to. He's a top gaelic footballer at home and he brings those skills to the soccer and rugby on tour too. I room with John Boy a lot on tour and he always brings his dart board with him. He's a huge fan of Liverpool – I can't watch a game on TV with him if 'pool are playing.

GEORGE DOCKRELL
Somerset, 36 caps, 16 ODIs

Dockers is probably the stupidest clever person in the world. He asks questions all the time – even when there's no point in asking a question. But he's a brilliant student and got a ridiculous 480 points in the Leaving Cert. He also has the strangest eating technique, which he does with his elbows spread wide, examining every morsel before he eats it.

I roomed with him in Dubai for the 2010 twenty20 qualifiers and he has the extremely annoying habit of turning on his iPod dock when I'm watching TV. He's a lovely guy, but the loudest 18-year-old we've ever had in the team. He's been in the team more than a year and has settled in well. When I was that age I didn't say boo to any of the senior guys, but Dockers just strolls into the dressing room and takes anyone's seat.

TRENT JOHNSTON
Railway Union, 138 caps, 47 ODIs

TJ's a close friend now that we've played together for Railway since 2007. He's been a huge player for Ireland, and seems to be getting better with age. He's a good lad around the changing room although he's a useless footballer – not surprising for a Newcastle fan.

He oversees the fines committee, and rules it with an iron fist. There's an element of discipline in it – you get fined for being late for the bus or a meeting – but a lot of it is just sadism. Everyone gets close to the max, which is about €15. It goes into a kitty which we spend on presents for people, like our liaison guy Shirish Buch, or just on a team night.

You get fined for stupid comments, or if you blow your top about something – TJ's always fining Simmo for blowing up at small things, or if he's in a bad mood. Keeping your head down and saying nothing isn't an option either, as you then get fined for being a 'church mouse'.

BOYD RANKIN
Warwickshire, 47 caps, 23 ODIs

Boydo is a typical farmer, a big 'goober' as they say up north. He's a lovely guy, big into his trance music, though he's also keen on Rihanna. He's an atrocious rugby player, and not too good at the soccer either. As a bowler he has improved enormously in the last few years and gives a world-class edge to our attack.

NIGEL JONES (left)
CSNI, 21 caps, 11 ODIs

ALBERT VAN DER MERWE (right)
YMCA, 12 caps, 8 ODIs

Jonesey and Albert are genuine, nice guys, and it was a hard time for them out in India as they never got to play a game. In the last World Cup everyone got a run at least once, but the format this time meant that just wasn't possible – which was a pity for them. They got a lot out of the trip though, and the experience they got being around the squad and taking part in the training will help them kick on.

Jonesy's a quiet lad, and he's been in team just over a year. He and Albert were enthusiastic members of the fines committee and Albie was regularly seen making notes of offences on his phone as they happened. But they were fantastic team men and always available and willing to do anything for you. If you needed some extra throw-downs or someone to feed a bowling machine they'd always put their hands up. If Boydo was the worst rugby player, Jonesy was definitely the worst footballer.

PHIL SIMMONS
Coach, 26 tests, 143 ODIs (West Indies)

Simmo is a really nice guy but don't get on wrong side of him if he's in bad mood. Or Spurs lose.

He's a great coach – everyone's game has stepped up since he took over after the 2007 World Cup. Since then I've got a lot fitter, which is a lot to do with the regime he's put in place. I've made a few small adjustments to my game since he arrived, and he's really good on working on different areas to score and new approaches.

Simmo's coaching record is unbelievable with Ireland, and he's great crack too, but one thing he's useless at is singing. He's terrible. He sits on the bus with his earphones in trying to sing along with Alicia Keyes and it all comes out out-of-tune and off-key. I thought I'd see him at the Rihanna gig when she played in Dublin last year but I believe he wasn't allowed go!

He doesn't play in the daily touch rugby games, but he's an enthusiastic line judge – even though he doesn't know the laws. He's getting into rugby though, and has become a regular at Leinster's games in the RDS and Lansdowne Road.

ROY TORRENS
Manager, 30 caps

Big Roy is a legend of Irish cricket – a seriously good fast bowler in his day and a nice man who'll do anything for you. He's the one we plague for flight bookings or lifts, and he always does it with a smile. He's been very helpful to mum and dad too, and great to have a pint with on tour when he relaxes and brings out his enormous fund of stories.

He's great around the dressing room, too, but don't ever watch a close game alongside him – he gets very jumpy.

Roy was a top soccer player in his day, and is still a huge Man U fan. After the World Cup a few us were invited out onto the Lansdowne Road pitch at half-time in Leinster's Heineken Cup quarter-final – and Roy confessed it was the first rugby match he had ever attended!

After I hit 12 sixes in an innings in Nairobi in 2008, Roy bet me that I wouldn't reach 100. I finished the World Cup with 95 so I hope he has to pay out before he finishes as manager, which he threatened to do at the end of the 2011 summer. He's going to be impossible to replace.

PETE JOHNSTON
Assistant Coach & Video Analyst

I played alongside Pete for Railway Union for three or four years and he's excellent at his job. We get fair amount of time off on tour, but you never see Pete because he gets very little down-time.

He does a huge amount of work – he goes to all training and games, and then does long hours in his room analysing the videos of our opponents as well as us. Anytime we have a team meeting he sets up a presentation to show us. The day before every game he'd have a short film on each of their batters and bowlers – showing their strengths, weaknesses, how they get out, where they hit fours.

I'd regularly go to him and ask him to pull up videos of, say, the Zimbabwe tour when I was playing well, or a particular innings against our next opponents. And Pete would email them to you, or you'd go to his room to watch them with him.

KIERAN O'REILLY
Physiotherapist

Kieran – or Ron as we call him – took over from Knoxy in 2008. He fits in well as he's just one of the lads as well as a very good physio. He looks after the Dublin senior gaelic footballers too.

If you go to him with a niggle he can tell you very quickly what's wrong – and what to do about it to make it better. Trent has benefited enormously from his skill, as he's hardly had an injury over the last two years. A lot of that is down to Kieran treating the niggles in time.

BRENDAN CONNOR
Strength and conditioning coach

Brendan is new to the Irish set up as he's just starting his career. He knows his stuff and works us hard. He's a quiet lad, but has definitely made a difference – he lives in Belfast but comes down to work with us three days a week.

BARRY CHAMBERS
Media manager

I don't know what we'd do without Barry, the man who can sort *anything* out. He works really hard and has been a great help as Irish cricket has made fast progress.

After the England match in Bangalore he was my first line of defence as I was under siege from the world's media. Barry took plenty of bullets for me that week. He and Roy make a great double act in a late night bar too!

There's just one guy missing off this list, of course, but I thought I'd leave him till last...

KEVIN O'BRIEN
Railway Union, 136 caps, 52 ODIs

I suppose you know all about me by this stage in the book. I go to the cinema quite often, and I also like rap, especially Eminem, and general chart music, especially Jay-Z and Alicia Keyes – she's class.

I must confess that I hadn't read very many books since I left school, except TJ and Siggo's excellent *'Raiders of the Caribbean'* about the last World Cup, of course! Last summer I got into reading again, thanks to a recommendation from my girlfriend Ruth-Anne Kilty. She told me about these great thrillers by a Swedish author and I was instantly hooked. I devoured the Stieg Larsson trilogy – I was even reading him while I was waiting to bat in Canada. Since then I've read a lot of thrillers, mainly by James Patterson, and am now into this Danish guy Jø Nesbo.

Besides that I'm a home-loving boy from Sandymount who likes to hit a cricket ball as far as he can.

HIT THE DECK:
Railway's defeat to Merrion in the Irish Senior Cup final was very disappointing

CHAPTER 6
WINTER WONDER

WHEN A CRICKET SEASON ENDS YOU USUALLY GET A FEW months to wind down. I usually play a bit of social hockey in Railway and just chill out. But the autumn and winter before the World Cup was crazy, playing cricket on four continents.

The first week in September saw us travel to Canada where we won an Intercontinental Cup game and two ODIs – where Paul Stirling set a new Irish record of 177 with a great display of hitting.

Then it was back to Dublin for the Bob Kerr Irish Senior Cup final, which was ruined by rain. We made 317 for 3, with TJ and I making rapid 70s, but the rules of the competition were barmy and Merrion just had to make 129 in 25 overs which they did easily enough. That was a great disappointment.

We didn't have time to mope, though, as we were then off to Zimbabwe for a short tour. The four-day game was a draw, mainly because the wicket was one of the flattest I've ever played on. They got 590, which we weren't happy to hear was the highest score anyone had ever made against Ireland.

We also had three ODIs, and they were all close games, with Zimbabwe winning the series 2-1. I was happy with my form there, scoring a few runs and getting six wickets sharing the new ball with TJ.

The travel continued in early October when I got an invitation to attend the ICC Cricket Awards.

These are a major event on the cricket calendar and it was especially nice to be short-listed for Associate & Affiliate Cricketer of the Year alongside Mohammed Shahzad (Afghanistan), Ryan ten Doeschate (Holland) and Trent.

Ruth-Anne and I headed over to India with TJ and his wife Vanessa, and the trip was especially interesting as the event was held in the ITC Royal Gardenia in Bangalore – which was going to be our home for ten days in the following March. It is comfortably the nicest hotel I'm ever stayed in, and the trip was a fantastic taste of what we had to come.

It was also my first taste of how much India loves cricket and it was a complete eye-opener. Nialler had told me all about his time in the ICL with the Delhi Jets and warned me that there was nowhere to escape cricket. He says you just can't understand how big a sport cricket is until you go to India.

The hotel was mobbed with all the great names and there was a fantastic buzz about the place. 'TenDo' won the award but the four Irish guests had a great time too.

Our preparation for the World Cup began in earnest a few weeks later when we headed for India.

We spent the first three weeks in November at a high-intensity training camp in the city of Pune. It was the best preparation for a tournament we have ever had – everything was looked after from fitness to nutrition and the quality of facilities and opposition.

We were based at the Pune Sports Club and were very well looked after. Five nets were available to us every day and 20 good local bowlers to help us work on our game.

It was an interesting trip for two men in particular – Ed Joyce and Hamish Marshall – who were new to the Irish set-up under Phil Simmons. In fact the two of them had played *against* Ireland in the 2007 World Cup! It was my first time to play and train with them – Ed had left the Irish scene to play for England by the time I was first capped and Hamish had just recently qualified after playing 13 tests and 66 ODIs for New Zealand.

I knew Hamish from my days with MCC, when I roomed with Shaun O'Brien, an English guy who is no relation! Shaun's parents live in Auckland and when he's there he plays in the same club as the Marshalls.

Hamish came up to London to stay a few times and we got on well. I had met Ed a few times when I was with Notts – but I knew a lot about him as he was Irish cricket's biggest star for many years.

It was fantastic to have two top class players joining our squad – just watching them train was a great help. It was fascinating to see how much time they have for the ball, and how well they hit it. Their experience is also valuable to us – they've been in so many situations so many times that they know instinctively how to play every time. Sharing that with us was brilliant. They brought a lot to the squad over those three weeks.

KIWI CONVERT:
Hamish Marshall was very influential on us before he even played

Our days in Pune started really early – 6am – which was when we had our yoga session with a local instructor. She showed us lots of useful techniques and it definitely helped with flexibility, and strengthening core muscles and legs.

The whole trip got us really fit, and opened our eyes to what conditions are like in the sub-continent.

We arrived at 6pm in the evening and the temperature was 30 degrees, and very humid. A few of us muttered to each other that if it was so hot and sticky in the evening, what would it be like in the middle of the day?

We brought 20 players with us, and we divided into two groups – one spent the morning doing fitness while they other worked on cricket skills. After lunch we switched around. It was hard work but very satisfying, and we also played three games against local teams which put into practice what we had worked on in nets.

When we got back home we soon regretted all that complaining about the weather in India. The contrast couldn't have been greater as Ireland was buried under snow for most of December. At one stage it got so deep that it proved impossible to drive to training in North County, and when the gym in Dublin City University was closed I had an early Christmas holiday!

I kept working on my own and went for daily runs through Sandymount and around Railway Union in a couple of inches of snow. It did look magical, but I remember thinking to myself that there wouldn't be much of that where we were heading.

At the end of January we again upped our preparation for the World Cup with a trip to the Global Cricket Academy in Dubai. By the time we left I was gagging for some cricket again.

The GCA is based at the Sports City Stadium and has facilities that are second to none. A few us went there before the World Twenty20 in 2010 for special programmes with three top coaches who all had long Test careers – Australian wicketkeeper Rod Marsh, Kiwi bowler Dayle Hadlee and Pakistani batsman Mudassar Nazar. I spent a lot of time on that trip working on my bowling with Dayle, a very good coach who is famous for producing Shane Bond.

We had access to the main stadium, two other grounds and a massive indoor school with eight lanes for batting and bowling. Four of the lanes had special machines to simulate different types of bowling – a standard machine bowling varieties of pace, Merlin, which bowls spin, and Iron Mike, which has a rotating arm. They also had this fantastic new device called Pro-Batter, which uses real match film to simulate the bowler running up past the stumps. It is really close to a match situation, with an umpire, crowds, the lot. I spent a lot of time facing "Tim Bresnan" – or a film of him – where "Tim" would run up and deliver, and the ball would come at you out of a hole in the screen where his hand was. It was class – Simmo fell in love with the machine, but it's very expensive.

There was an amazing attention to detail – the soil in the main stadium comes from India, while in the other two grounds half the pitches are from India, half from Perth in Australia. This gives teams the chance to

ROCKY XI: *Boxing has become part of our exercise programme: here Porty and Ed Joyce spar*

simulate pitch conditions before a tour, for example. There were 35 nets in the main ground, with soil from the sub-continent, England and Australia.

We played a couple of practice games against Kenya and Zimbabwe, which was hard for us coming in cold from indoor training at home – they were playing in the middle of their summers and beat us.

Then we moved on to Nagpur in India for the first of the official World Cup warm-up games against New Zealand and Zimbabwe. Everything changed when we touched down in India – the time spent at training increased, and the intensity we went about it increased too.

We always seem to play New Zealand in warm-ups and World Cups – and we *never* play well against them. The always get big scores against us. This time we ran them close, and could have won. It was a flat wicket and we dropped their opening batsman Martin Guptill – who got 130 – and the rest batted around him to get 311.

BACK IN BLACK:
Bowling against New Zealand in a warm-up game in Nagpur

We got off to flying start and were 85 off 10 overs, with Stirlo batting really well on 39 off 35 balls. Then their skipper, Daniel Vettori, brought himself on and he was the only difference between us. Most of the batters got some time in the middle and made a few runs against the rest of the bowlers, but Vettori took 4-42 off his 10 and that was the key.

It had been a huge improvement on the Dubai games and Phil was very happy afterwards, but our next game was against Zimbabwe who we had played four or five times over the winter.

We completely dominated them – TJ and Boyd blew away the top order to have them reeling on 12 for 3. We dropped their skipper Elton Chigumbura on 30 and he went on to make 100, so we ended up chasing 245 when we should have had them out for well under 200.

I was struggling for runs and when I went in, at 127 for 4, I felt a bit of pressure. I was the only one of the top six not to have a good score in the warm-ups. Andre Botha and I put on 99 in 15 overs which got us close to victory, which came pretty easily in the end. I made 62 off 61 balls which calmed me down again. The last thing you need is to go into a World Cup with no runs behind you.

We then headed off to Bangladesh, where the opening ceremony took place on 17 February. India were on our flight from Nagpur to Dhaka, and sitting in the VIP lounge watching Sachin Tendulkar, Virender Sehwag and company was a reminder that we were now in the big time.

The opening ceremony was a bit of crack, with Porty being wheeled around in a rickshaw, but the rest of our stay in Dhaka wasn't quite as exciting.

The trouble was that our first game wasn't scheduled until eight days after the World Cup started – and it got more difficult to watch matches on TV while we were waiting to get going. We were the last team to start their programme, and we were playing the hosts who had already played India. Kenya played twice before we played even once – and when they were skittled in both games the anti-associates grumbling had started.

We trained every day, which eventually became boring as we had nothing else to break up the day. Security was very heavy and we were told we could not leave the hotel. The consolation was that there were two shops selling DVDs in the hotel – and they only charged $1 per disc. A few of the guys stocked up on box sets, which were great value. My TV taste is a bit girly I'm afraid – I love the American high school shows. I picked up stuff like *Californication, Beverly Hills 90210, Gossip Girl* and *Glee!*

There's often little else to do in the hotel except watch TV or read, so we usually swap DVDs around the squad. Willo loves *Grey's Anatomy*, while George Dockrell and Paul Stirling are big fans of *Prison Break*.

So, as you can imagine, that first game couldn't have come any sooner.

A NEW STAR:
George Dockrell bowled magnificently for a teenager in his first World Cup match

CHAPTER 7
IRELAND VERSUS
BANGLADESH

WE HAD PLAYED IN BANGLADESH BEFORE, BUT THIS OPENING match of our 2011 World Cup was very different. There were 35,000 people crammed into the Sher-e-Bangla Stadium and no more than half-a-dozen were supporting Ireland. There was one guy from County Clare, James Carolan, living there with his family, while the Bangladeshi Clontarf player Ropu came along with his Irish fiancée.

It wasn't their fault, but we didn't hear much of the Irish contingent when we were out on the park. Bangladesh started well and they got the crowd on their side from the start.

From ball one you couldn't hear a thing – they started well as Boyd struggled to get his rhythm and after five overs they were 49 for 0. It's hard for opening bowlers these days – the tracks are always batsman-friendly and teams now attack the new ball from the start. Boyd and TJ saw how if you're even a tiny bit off your length you're gone. Mudassar Nazar told us in Dubai that the best time to score runs on the sub-continent is when the ball is new and coming on to the bat – it is much harder to get it through the infield when the ball gets soft.

John Boy came on early and did well, and my brother Niall silenced the crowd with a stunning leg-side stumping to dismiss Imrul Keyes. The first example of our new improved fielding came when Ed Joyce hit the stumps direct from midwicket to dismiss Junaid Siddique, and when André had Tamim Iqbal caught at point they were in trouble on 73 for 3 off 12 overs. When the skipper was out caught and bowled by André the crowd went completely quiet.

But Mushfiqur and Raqibul put on about 60 but then Dockers started to turn the screw and grabbed a couple of wickets. For a guy playing his first World Cup game he was unbelievable, and his figures of 9-2-23- 2 had

WATER CARRIERS: *Albert van der Merwe and Nigel Jones were a key part of the squad without ever playing a game*

the commentators in ecstasy. André, who had been so brilliant against Pakistan four years earlier, ended with 3 for 32.

Bangladesh were lucky to get 200 in the end – and when you consider their blistering start that means we had kept them to 155 off the last 45 overs. That is exceptional, and hugely down to our brilliant fielding.

We were excited during the break, as we all knew that 205 was very gettable – this was exactly the start we needed.

We came out and there was a new challenge for us – the floodlights were on. We had only batted once before under lights – against New Zealand in Nagpur – but these conditions were very different. The atmosphere in Mirpur was hazy and dirty, and as night fell the dew was heavy.

We had spent a lot of time practising under lights, as several World Cup games would be played in the evening. Floodlights are good nowadays so there's no worry about not being able to see the ball, as used to be the case.

BANGLADESH

The one thing that is different from daytime games is when the ball is skied up into the air when you're fielding. There's a danger that you lose the flight of the ball when it goes into the lights and if you're hit by the glare it takes three seconds to refocus your eyes.

When we started to bat William hit a lovely four in the first over, and the Bangladesh skipper responded immediately by bringing his spinners on. Razzaq tied us down for a bit, but Stirlo was very unlucky when the ball hit his foot and rolled back to the keeper, who stumped him. The Bangladesh spinners turned the screw and the crowd got involved again.

It was around then my nerves kicked in. I'm usually quite chilled out waiting my turn to bat, but this time I was in a total heap. I couldn't watch the game live so I retreated into the back of the dressing room to watch it on TV. That didn't really help. The TV pictures were broadcast four seconds later than live, but I could hear the screams and cheers from the crowd – and the guys – as the action happened. I'd be watching the bowler running in and the crowd would be roaring, and then you'd hear our players outside cheering. I stopped watching then – I couldn't watch it. There I was with my head in my hands all on my own, with just Boyd in the back room having an ice bath.

When I was next in I walked into players' gallery – but the nerves got even worse waiting to bat. It was definitely the most nervous I have ever been. In one way I was glad it didn't last too long as Whitey was out for 10. As I walked out to join Niall I looked up and saw the scoreboard reading 93 for 4. There was still a long way to go.

Nialler was batting brilliantly, taking his time and hitting everything loose. I was sure he would be there at the end but he was out to an amazing catch. He tried to tuck away a single on the leg side but got a bit much on it and chipped it to square leg. Tamim charged in from the boundary and dived forward full length to catch the ball millimetres off the ground.

We needed less than 100 but our top five were all back in the hutch.

André came in to join me and after we played ourselves in we went on the attack. I took a liking to Mohammed Ashraful and hit my first six of the tournament, though he almost got me out with one of his funny double bouncers.

Shakib-al-Hasan read the conditions really well, as you would expect, and constantly changed his bowlers around. But I'm convinced it was changing the ball that proved the turning point. As in the first innings it became discoloured and the umpires allowed them to change to a whiter ball, which was supposed to be of otherwise similar condition.

The skipper brought back their best seam bowler, Shafiul Islam, and the ball suddenly started seaming around again. The ball was perfectly white and he was bowling classic away swingers which he had no right to be bowling with a 30-over-old ball. That changed the game as far as I'm concerned, and how he didn't get the man of the match award for his spell of 4 for 10 off six overs I will never know.

Still, with 14 overs left we needed exactly four an over. Shafiul bowled me a long hop and I had a go but I picked out the fielder at deep square leg. If it had gone five yards either side of the fielder it was a four.

I got a bit of stick in the media, with some people saying that was a bad shot to play – but it was instinctive. It was a pity I dragged it out to the fielder, and looking back I should have hit it for one. That shot where I pick the ball up over mid-wicket is a strength of mine – five days later I played it against Tim Bresnan and hit him into the stand.

John Boy was very nervous, too, and just never settled, and after that the innings just petered out and we were all out for 175 with five overs unused.

The dressing room was quiet afterwards, a lot of guys had their heads down – we just didn't believe we hadn't chased down the runs. Then Simmo walked in and said "I don't want to see any heads down. We have five more games and we walk out of here with our chests out and head high. We can

TUNNEL VISION: *Paul Stirling and William Porterfield get ready to start the chase*

still win all five – we can qualify. Forget about the defeat and let's learn from what we did wrong."

The journey back to the hotel helped take our minds off the match. We had made the trip in less than 20 minutes every previous occasion, but that night it took an hour and a half as we stopped three or four times as the police tried to clear a way through thousands of happy Bangladeshis going bonkers in the street. We inched through a crowd of 100,000 people as they danced and cheered. Bangladesh were under a lot of pressure after they'd been hammered by India – so I don't know what they'd have done if we'd have beaten them. Later in the tournament they stoned the West Indies bus after they had beaten their heroes.

THE MOMENT:
My first hundred in a World Cup – and it's the fastest one anyone has ever made

CHAPTER 8
IRELAND VERSUS ENGLAND

BANGALORE WAS MY FAVOURITE CITY OF ALL THOSE WE VISITED during the World Cup. The city and its eight million people were very friendly and welcoming, and the security was non-existent compared to the other venues. We were at last allowed out of the hotel and it was great to have a chance to stroll around the centre of the city.

It was also the phase of the competition when we had most support from home – it was the easiest of the venues to get to and our two biggest games were there in the space of a week. There were a lot fewer supporters than in the West Indies four years before, but India is a lot harder to get to and the economic recession had also helped reduce the numbers of those able to travel.

There was a great buzz around the ITC Royal Gardenia, especially when several of the wives and girlfriends of the squad arrived. It didn't take long to forget Bangladesh. Porty, Stirlo and a few of the lads went to see England play India, but I just hung around the pool and then watched the last five overs – which turned out to be the interesting part. It was a classic game of cricket and even in the short time I was watching England had it won, then India had it won – and then neither of them won as the game finished in an incredible 338-338 tie.

The next day saw a visit to the Bounce hair salon around the corner from the hotel. It wasn't just the team wanting to look their best before the big games; there was a serious element to the trip. The TodayFM radio station had been running their 'Shave or Dye' campaign, which aimed to increase awareness of cancer and raise funds for research. A couple of guys in the squad were very keen that we help out and we were all delighted to join in. Everyone made a donation to the campaign and the few guys that backed out had to pay $25 into the fund.

Phil Simmons had his head shaved and his goatee dyed blue, while John Boy, André Botha and TJ went for a No 1 cut. Joyce and Nialler had boring highlights done, but it was myself, Boyd and Porty that really got into the mood. Boyd went for a bleached spiky top, while Porty decided to dye his hair purple. For some reason I reckoned that a peroxide blond cut with shocking pink highlights was the way to go. My girlfriend Ruth-Anne hated it but it certainly helped make me stand out for the rest of the trip!

I met Ruth-Anne in Railway years ago but we only started going out in the summer of 2010. She told me that she had watched the 2007 World Cup in Nice, where she was studying on the Erasmus programme and working in Wayne's Irish Bar.

Later that night Ruth-Anne and I joined Nialler in the bar for a couple of cokes – as is the norm before a game – when in walked England players Graeme Swann, James Anderson and Tim Bresnan. I know Swanny quite well having played alongside him for Notts, and they came over to take the mickey about the haircuts. They were slagging Nialler, too, because he hadn't been as outrageous as I had.

The day of March 2nd dawned and I noticed I wasn't half as nervous as I had been before Bangladesh. We had breakfast in the hotel – the usual scrambled eggs, bacon, toast and a few cups of tea.

There was a different atmosphere around the guys when we got to ground, and everyone seemed much more relaxed. The tension started to build when we went out to practice 90 minutes before the start and I saw Mum, Dad and Ruth-Anne up in the stand above the dressing room. It was a bit of a blow when André broke down during the warm-up – I didn't even know he had a niggle.

All the talk before the game was about England's tie with India, and how Andrew Strauss's 158 was one of the greatest innings ever seen.

In Boyd's third over Strauss top-edged the ball down to Dockers at fine leg, but just when it looked like he was going to catch it the ball just kept

KNEE TROUBLE: *Kieran works his magic after a nasty bang fielding in Bangalore. Albert, TJ and Willo look concerned*

sailing over his head for six. We had been told that Bangalore was 3,000 feet above sea-level and the air was thus much thinner.

During the seventh over Strauss crashed a drive out to me at cover and I stopped it, but fumbled it. As I was falling I reached for the ball and my studs slipped in the turf. I went over on my ankle and my knee took a ferocious bang as I hit the ground.

I was rolling around in agony when our physio Kieran O'Reilly came running out. Ron manoeuvred it around and sprayed some freezing agent on it. At first I thought it was serious, maybe even the end of the tournament for me, but after a bit I felt better and told him "it's not too bad, I'll get up." It was tender for a while, and I especially felt it when I pushed off in the field, but after about 10 overs I forgot about it.

Although I'd been bowling well in the nets, I didn't bowl against England. We've a side full of bowlers – only Ed, Niall and Porty don't turn their arm over – so somebody has to miss out. As an all-rounder I always

PROUD AS PUNCH: *Mum and Dad were interviewed on the legendary BBC Test Match Special. This is them in the commentary box*

like to contribute in the field, but if the skipper doesn't call on me it doesn't bother me.

England were batting easily and knocked up their 50 in eight overs, and were cruising on 91 for 0 in the 14th over. Dockers had started well, and was rewarded when Andrew Strauss missed a straight one – the England captain out for 34 on his 34th birthday.

While all the talk beforehand was about Kevin Pietersen's weakness against left-arm spin, it wasn't George who dismissed him – it was Stirlo's offies. KP tried to be a bit clever with a reverse dab and the ball looped up to Nialler. That left England on 111 for 2 but it was 167 runs later that we celebrated our next scalp after Jonathan Trott and Ian Bell tucked in. Mooners came back to dismiss both of them and he and TJ kept it very tight at the end. They kept picking up wickets and stopped them from scoring with back-of-a-length slower balls. They only made 70 off the last ten overs and a total that looked like it might be 360 was down to 327. It was still a lot, but less than England had made against India on the same ground.

At half-time we talked about how we had chased 317 against New Zealand in the warm-up, and how we didn't have to be reckless and aim for 100 off the first 10 overs. We have plenty of batting down the order with the likes down of John Boy and TJ coming in 8 and 9. We reckoned we just needed a solid foundation from the top order: aim to be around 50 for 0 off the first 10 overs and play from there.

That plan was out the window after the first ball, which was passing harmlessly wide of off stump when Porty dragged it back onto his wicket. Stirlo continued to play his usual attacking game and hit some great shots off Broad and Anderson before he top-edged Bresnan for 32.

Joycey and Niall batted brilliantly, and comfortably sailed past the 100 when Swann bowled Nialler for 29. It was a shame, as he was hitting it very cleanly and revels in those situations. Ed was out stumped soon after and then Willo went and the score of 111 for 5 didn't look so hot.

Our media manager Barry Chambers told me later that he looked around the press room at that stage and saw that a lot of the English journalists were starting to write their final reports and planning where they were going to eat that night. Others were updating their Facebook pages.

Alex Cusack joined me at the wicket and we chatted about the match situation and how we needed to take our time but stay positive. I whacked Michael Yardy for a couple of boundaries to get going.

Phil Simmons has given me licence to play my shots, which is great because I love hitting the ball hard and high. That's how cricket should be played. The wicket was extremely flat and the Chinnaswamy Stadium one of the smallest we played in, which meant we could pierce the infield or hit cleanly over them.

Before the next over I went up the Cusy for a chat. Graeme Swann had been bowling well – 7-0-26-3 at that stage – but I had faced him a lot in Nottingham and reckoned I could take him apart.

Cusy took a single off the third ball and I hit the next one into the cheap seats where the Indian fans went bonkers. I hit the last ball of the over in the same area too. That brought me to 25 off 14 balls and I started to feel I had a special score in me. The England bowlers were starting to get a bit frustrated and, just after I got to fifty, James Anderson bowled a ball at my feet. I got my bat down on it just in time.

"Good ball Jimmy", I said to him.

Anderson's face darkened and snapped back "What would you know what a good ball is?"

"Well I mightn't know what a good ball is," I came back with, "but I know a bad one. I just hit your last one over there," as I pointed my bat towards the grandstand.

They weren't happy. Matt Prior came up and told me to be quiet and I told him "if he's going to give me rubbish, I'll give it back."

"Just keep batting," he said.

"Yeah, I will," I said.

And I did.

Off the last ball of the next over I hit Tim Bresnan for a six over extra-cover, and the ball clattered into a motorbike that was there as part of a sponsor's promotion. There was a drinks break at the end of the over and Stuart Broad came up and put his arm around me and pointed at the bike, and says "that's yours, mate!"

I was puzzled and asked him, "what do you mean?"

"If you hit the bike, you get to keep it," he said. And I believed him!

"Happy days!", I grinned, and when Albert and Whitey came out with the drinks I was delighted to show them my new Hero Honda. Sadly, I'm still waiting for it to arrive.

CUSACK STAND: *Alex's innings was crucial in our match-winning partnership*

I heard afterwards that the rest of the guys were very relieved when the drinks interval arrived. Cricketers are very superstitious, and once someone gets going with the bat you're not allowed move out of your seat. They were glued to their benches for hours and could only take a loo break during the drinks intervals.

Next over I faced four balls from Anderson, which went four, four, dot, six. The last hit sailed quite a few rows back in the stand to the left of the press box. I didn't notice the replay on the screen and it was only later I discovered that it had travelled 102 metres – the biggest six of the tournament at the time.

Cusy was fantastic, running for everything and giving me plenty of strike. We put on 62 off the five over batting powerplay, which was 20 more than England had got off ours.

Ian Bell chipped in with some more nonsense like "lot of pressure on the big man. Don't throw it away now, Kevvy, you've a lot to lose".

I said "sorry mate, we've nothing to lose. We're little old Ireland and you're the big test team – you shouldn't be losing to us!"

With about 12 overs to go I knew we had it won. We needed about seven an over and there was always a four to be hit every over. England just didn't have an answer – they didn't know what they were up to with their bowling plans.

The fact that I could be on-course for a World Cup century didn't really register until I was dropped by Strauss on 91. It was then I told myself to pull my head in. They had five men on the boundary and the other four inside the ring were all on the edge of it. It was the easiest thing in the world to just block the ball and take the singles.

BIG HIT: *One of my six maximums in Bangalore*

When I was on 98 I was facing Yardy and tried to push the ball for one, and again Matt Prior chirped up from behind the stumps: "He's playing for his hundred, big Kev's playing for his hundred."

And I turned to him and said "wouldn't you?"

The next ball was a full toss which I clipped away to leg, and as soon as I hit it I shouted "two, two".

Up in the commentary box the former Indian legend Ravi Shastri must have heard me say it on stump mic, because I was barely halfway down the wicket for the first run when he said "...and he's coming back for two."

I turned straight away and kept the head down. I knew I was safe because I saw Broad had still another 15 yards to get to the ball. I just stretched my arms out, put my head in the air and screamed!

The English fielders didn't say anything to me then. Whitey told me

OH BROTHER, WHERE ART THOU: *Niall and I enjoy the buzz after the win over England. You can see from my eyes I'm still a bit zonked!*

afterwards that no-one on the opposition had clapped the hundred. I don't know why. I don't really care.

I saluted the dressing room and then looked up at the stand perched above it where I knew my parents and Ruth-Anne were sitting – they were on the big screen more than I was! Anytime I looked up at the screen while I was batting Mum was there shying away from the camera, and Dad was loving it!

Cusy, who made a brilliant 47 in a match-winning partnership of 162, sacrificed his wicket soon afterwards. John Boy then outscored me in a quick stand of about 40. I was run out trying to turn a one into a two – in an ideal world it would have been good if I had been there at the end to hit the winning runs, but it wasn't to be. I had no doubts that John Boy and TJ would see us home.

As the adrenaline stopped pumping I felt drained as I walked off, and headed into the dressing room to watch us try to get the last 11 runs on the TV. As I was taking my pads off I saw Broad at the top of his run-up getting ready to bowl to Trent.

THE INNINGS BALL BY BALL

Ball	Runs
23rd (Swann)	0400
24th (Yardy)	00
25th (Swann)	
(Wilson out)	
26th (Yardy)	14040
27th (Swann)	606
28th (Broad)	0040
29th (Swann)	0041
30th (Broad)	1
31st (Anderson)	0
32nd (Yardy)	00044
33st (Anderson)	0260
(FIFTY)	
34th (Bresnan)	416
35th (Anderson)	4406
36th (Yardy)	4
37th (Bresnan)	0046
38th (Collingwood)	102
39h (Yardy)	0
40th (Collingwood)	4
41st (Yardy)	102
(HUNDRED)	
42nd (Broad)	01
(Cusack out)	
43rd (Bresnan)	1
44th (Broad)	121
45th (Bresnan)	0
46th (Broad)	11
47th (Bresnan)	2
48th (Anderson)	11
49th (Broad)	1
(O'Brien out)	

6s: 6 (36 runs)
4s: 13 (52 runs)
2s: 5 (10 runs)
1s: 15 (15 runs)
0s: 24
Faced: 63 balls

Suddenly from outside the guys were shouting "great shot TJ!"

That irritating four second delay again! I couldn't stand it so I scampered back outside still wearing my thigh pad and box.

When John Boy slogged Anderson high into the sky, the whole squad stood up and followed the arc of the ball as it curved through the sky. One of the guys was commentating on it, saying "is it going to go, is it... is it..."

That was the last thing I heard because as soon as it bounced over the boundary we all erupted. We all just hopped on each other in one joyful mass of bodies. I remember seeing Albert, Whitey and Nigel Jones racing out to the middle to grab a souvenir stump.

We must have spent two or three minutes in that huddle before people started peeling away. There was no wall between the viewing areas for the two teams and just four feet away Andy Flower was sitting with Kevin Pietersen, who wasn't looking too happy.

I broke away and went over to shake their hands. Flower said "well batted" and KP just shook my hand. I think they were still a bit shocked.

I looked up at the grandstand where Mum, Dad and Ruth-Anne were waving and cheering. I think there were a few tears too.

SWEET VICTORY: Roy Torrens is rarely happier than when he has a cake in his hand, this one courtesy of our Bangalore hotel

CHAPTER 9
AFTERMATH

I BARELY HAD A MOMENT TO GET MY BREATH WHEN I WAS dragged in front of the camera for the post-game interview, the man of the match presentation, and the press conference. There were hundreds of media there, mostly from India, with quite a few from England and a handful of the Irish guys who cover us all the time. I was still a bit zonked.

I told them it was by a long, long way the best innings I've ever played, although I also told them I may have once scored more off Nialler in the garden back home in Sandymount.

The native media were all dying to hear whether I was interested in playing in their Indian Premier League, but I played a straight bat on that one. I just said I was only there to represent Ireland, but that I loved to hit the ball hard and how Twenty20 suits my game.

There were a couple of silly questions about my haircut, but before I finished I wanted to make one point that I thought was really important. We're a very united team, but there was naturally extra attention paid to the guys who played full-time pro cricket for counties. Cricket Ireland and RSA had introduced contracts for all the home-based players and that was crucial. I told the world's media about that, and how being able to train and rest when you need to is so important. It was no coincidence that five of the most prominent players in the win over England – Alex, George, Trent, Johnny and I – were all based at home.

My one regret was that because of all the attention I wasn't able to join the guys in the changing room for the start of the party. We then got on to the bus for the short scoot around to the hotel, and we saluted our opponents with a chorus of 'Are You Scotland in Disguise?'

When we arrived, the hotel manager very kindly presented me with a bat-shaped chocolate cake with the number '113' formed by hazelnuts. I was very touched, and the cake proved very popular, and delicious, about four o'clock in the morning as we all relaxed in Porty's room.

It was after midnight when we got back to the hotel so the bar was closing. We were having a few beers when Andrew Strauss walked through the lobby and we gave him a blast of 'Happy Birthday'. He gave us a big grin and came back down shortly afterwards with Matt Prior and Paul Collingwood and we all shared a couple of pints.

I woke about eight o'clock and headed down for breakfast but my knee was still sore. Kieran wasn't too happy to get a call to ask him to strap it up again, but I was a bit worried about it. It had swollen quite a bit and was still throbbing. To be fair to Ron he did a great job for a man with one hour of sleep under his belt!

When I switched on my phone it was ridiculous – more than 70 texts flooded in on my Irish number alone, and plenty more on the Indian mobile I hired for the month. I heard from guys I hadn't heard from since our schooldays, which was nice. I then turned on the laptop to find I had 487 emails from Facebook. There were dozens from Indian fans saying "you're my new favourite player, please come and play in the IPL". It took me three days to read them all.

And if I thought that the world of cricket would move on to the next game in the competition, I was sorely mistaken.

Once I'm up I can't go back to sleep, so I spent the morning lazing by the pool. I had my phone on silent and dozed off for half an hour. When I woke up there were 17 missed calls and four texts in just that half an hour. Our media manger Barry Chambers called up to say that there were interviews lined up for 10, 10.15, 10.30, 10.45 and 11 o'clock. At one stage he counted 132 formal requests: in the end I did thirty. It was great that so many people wanted to interview me, but I couldn't keep up.

It was great honour to get a phone call from President Mary McAleese

BROTHERS IN ARMS: *John Boy celebrates the win, while the picture on the wall from 2007 shows his brother Paul doing the same in Jamaica*

that afternoon. I talked to the President after the Pakistan game in 2007 so it was a double delight to get the call. She said some very nice things to me, and told me that I had made Irish people so proud. She told me my efforts were "Cuchulain-esque", which made me laugh. Cuchulain was the ancient Irish hero who killed a giant dog with one blow from a hurley. I thought that was a very funny thing to say.

The guys were all lounging around the hotel and picked up some of the local newspapers which were amazing. All the front pages had pictures of this guy in a green shirt, which seemed a bit surreal to me.

Some of the headlines made good puns about the haircut, although there seemed to be confusion about the colour. 'Pink flayed' was the front page headline on the *Deccan Times*, while the *Bangalore Mirror* ran with 'Purple reign'. *The Times of India* had a good one too: 'England Brien-dead', while the *Deccan Chronicle* screamed 'England sham, Ireland rocks'.

At the time there was a big international crisis in Libya, and there were 18,000 Indian citizens trying to get out of the country, but still the local TV stations thought my innings was the top story. I suppose it was then

I realised how much cricket dominates everything in India.

Nialler told me that as soon as he turned on his phone after the game he found he had already got a couple of enquiries from English counties and an Australian state about his little brother. There was a lot going on and my head was starting to hurt. Eventually I had to switch my phone on silent, and I was even dodging Barry.

At that stage Phil told me I wasn't to speak to the press, which was a big relief to me. I knew where Simmo was coming from, as I had just written a piece for the *Mail on Sunday* which they headlined 'I need to refocus'. I was getting so many calls and requests to do stuff that I wasn't focusing on the next game, which was the main reason we were in India. It wasn't just me, as the Indian media also wanted a piece of John Boy and Dockers and they were getting tugged around too.

> *There was a lot going on and my head was starting to hurt. Eventually I had to switch my phone on silent*

We were there to play cricket, everything else was a sideshow. For those two or three days I didn't prepare as well as I should have done. That was my own fault, but with so many requests for autographs, interviews and photos it is hard to say no. I was glad when Simmo brought in that media ban.

Barry forwarded me an interesting email from Matthew Hayden, the former Australian legend whose record for the fastest century in World Cups I had just beaten.

Haydos was a big hero of mine and it was fantastic to get his email. He had been off on a remote island working for his foundation on an educational programme with the tribes who live there, and so had missed the game and all the fuss afterwards.

He told me how he heard the news:

"Five minutes before the start of the Tiwi Island Land Council, the chairman Cyril Rioli stood and said, 'Hey Matty, did you hear about the Irish fella who broke your record overnight'.

"I said 'No, I didn't, tell me more'.

"Continuing he said, 'Yer this bloke almost single handed beat the English scoring 113 in the game and getting them out of trouble, pity about your record too', he added with a cheeky smile. 'He smashed your record beating it by 10 balls or something'.

"Well, I honestly couldn't believe it. It just didn't sink in that not only did you smash my record but you smashed the Poms as well, something Australia found so hard to do this summer in the Ashes.

"I trust that the remainder of the tournament goes particularly well for you all and wish you all the very best."

Sincerely, Matthew Hayden.

My birthday was on the Friday, which gave us a chance to escape from the hotel for a while. Niall, Ruth-Anne and I went over to the Pride Hotel where mum and dad were staying and the hotel put on a big spread for us. It wasn't the most spectacular birthday for presents: Ruth-Anne gave me a bag of sweets and Mum handed over a couple of lottery scratchcards from my big sister Ciara. And no, I didn't win!

IN DEMAND: *Ruth-Ann and TJ's wife Vanessa Johnston being interviewed by the Deccan Herald*

WHAT THEY SAID ABOUT KEVIN'S INNINGS...

Many times people bandy the word "great" around loosely, but this was one of the great one-day innings. Not only did O'Brien score his hundred off 50 balls with clean striking, he did it from a position when Ireland were losing the game and he finished up taking them to victory. That is an exceptional performance
English commentator Geoff Boycott

Its funny, when Ireland beat Pakistan in Jamaica, Niall was man of the match. Here in another historic win, Kevin has got man of the match. It feels great
Camilla O'Brien

It was an outstanding innings. The gall he showed taking the game to us... I can't take anything away from it. It was brilliant batting.
England captain Andrew Strauss

This is the greatest sporting day I've ever witnessed. It makes me so proud to be Irish, but also proud for all those many people who are involved in Irish cricket. There's men and women all over the country who played their part today, from those who coach the kids when they first take up the game to the people who give up so much time to look after grounds, umpire, write about it. This moment is for them
Ex-Ireland captain Alan Lewis

It's like England beating Ireland at hurling
Dublin Gaelic footballer Mossie Quinn

O'Brien was sensational. He did something which not even the best of teams and players had ever managed against the minnows. Here was a rank

AFTERMATH

outsider giving a serious hammering to one of the top teams at the World Cup. In one stroke he has ensured opponents have both respect and fear for Ireland
Indian legend Ravi Shastri

Nasser hussain jokes! Ireland no referals right out of 10 appeals. 1 key stat for u now bud: Eng beat by 3 wkts in Bangalore... chins
John Mooney's tweet to ex-England captain Nasser Hussein, now a Sky commentator

Every now and again someone wakes up and has the best day of their life - and yesterday Kevin O'Brien did that. We should have bowled better; we certainly could have bowled better, but that's tarnishing the knock he had - personally I think he won the game rather than we lost it
Graeme Swann

To be frank, it wasn't clear what the plan was. Perhaps they thought Ireland weren't good enough to hit length out of the park. If that was the thinking, it was clearly wrong
Former England captain Nasser Hussain

Some bookmakers had Ireland at 400-1 at one stage. I wish I'd not kept my money in pocket
Ger O'Brien

England made it easy for them with shoddy cricket. There was a palpable sense of complacency that crept in during the Ireland innings, born undoubtedly of arrogance and a ridiculous belief in their superiority. England were bad but take nothing away from Ireland; they played magnificently and courageously
Former England captain, Mike Atherton

INDIAN SUMMER:
Nialler batted brilliantly against the hosts before he was run out for 46

CHAPTER 10
IRELAND VERSUS INDIA

WE GOT AN IDEA OF WHAT IT MUST BE LIKE TO BE AN INDIAN cricketer two days before we played them. Most of the team just stayed in their rooms to keep away from the constant pestering of fans, but on the Friday one of the team walked into the hotel bar and the poor guy was instantly surrounded by about 20 people looking for autographs and photos. Although I was under siege myself around the same time, I also knew that it wouldn't last. These guys have this all the time. There's a story that Sachin Tendulkar can only drive his sports car around the streets of Mumbai between 3 and 4 o'clock in the morning.

Our usual match-day routine is to leave the hotel two hours before start of play, and we get a police escort to the ground. The Irish fans had to leave about ten minutes later and were still only settled in their seats with a few minutes to spare as the queues at the turnstiles wound miles down Mahatma Gandhi Road.

We usually head out for our warm-ups 90 minutes before the start and it was a bit shocking to see that the ground was almost full at that stage. It was the biggest crowd I have ever played in front of – there were 45,000 people there but

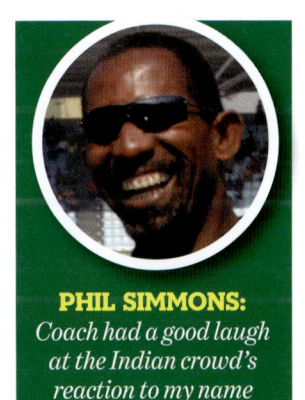

PHIL SIMMONS:
Coach had a good laugh at the Indian crowd's reaction to my name

they made the noise of twice that many. In terms of population, there are 240 Indians for every Irish person, and the proportions were pretty similar inside the stadium,

I was taking catches off Simmo when they called out the teams. 'Tendulkar... Sehwag... Gambhir...' every name was greeted with a huge roar. Then they started on our guys: 'Porterfield... Stirling... Joyce...' and the crowd cheered politely. But just as Simmo launched a ball towards me I heard my name being called out and this enormous roar came up, just as loud as for any Indian. I just stopped and looked at Phil and he had this huge grin on his face. I didn't know what to think, but I felt the hairs prickle on the back of my neck.

Our win over England had forced the Indians to change their plans. Mahendra Singh Dhoni told the press that he called a special team meeting to examine the Irish performance, and they felt they had to recall their spearhead Zaheer Khan, who they had planned to rest.

It was probably just as well that I didn't find out till afterwards that around one billion people watched the game, most of them in Asia.

Zaheer started really well and had Porty dropped third ball and bowled Stirlo off the next. When he got Joycey to edge one to the keeper next over, we were 9 for 2. Niall and William then batted really well, putting on over 100 in the next 20 overs before Nialler was run out for 46.

It was a completely different track to the game against England, a lot slower and with more turn for the spinners. We played well against the specialist spinners, Harbhajan Singh and Piyush Chawla, but it was the part-time all-rounder Yuvraj Singh that did the damage. He's such a take-him-for-granted sort of bowler that lots of sides underestimate him. He had a great World Cup with bat and ball and well deserved the Player of the Tournament award.

He certainly turned the screw against us and when he dismissed Whitey I was next in to bat. As I walked out to the middle I could hear the crowd going off their rocker again. And as I looked up to get used to the surroundings all I could see was 44,500 Indians – and 500 Irish – screaming at the top of their voices.

It was easier to concentrate than you might think. I have a few words that I use to help me focus. I watch the bowler running in and say a couple of words to myself that help me focus. After he bowls I chill out again, have a look around, and then say those words again. I find this 'switch on, switch

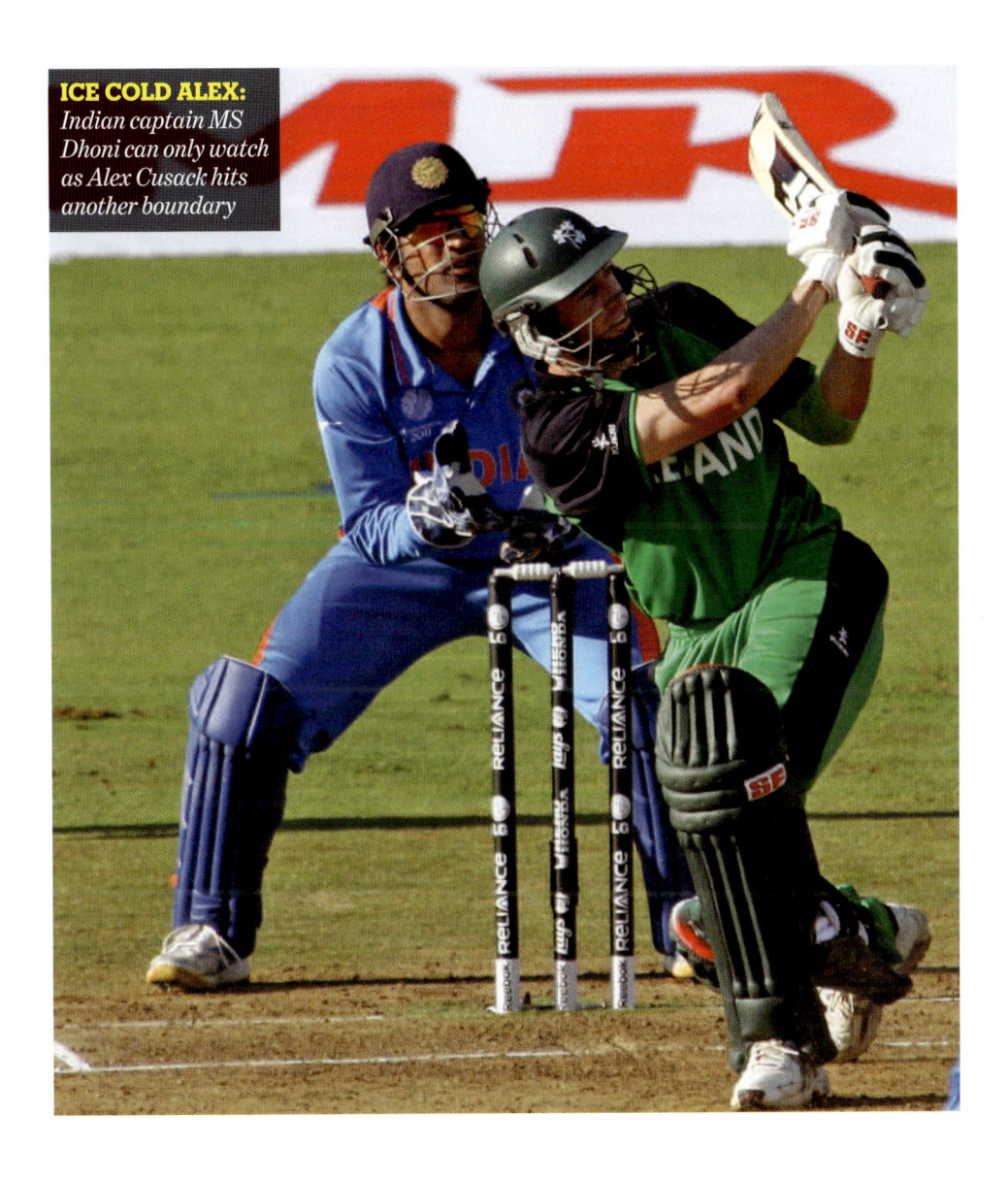

ICE COLD ALEX:
Indian captain MS Dhoni can only watch as Alex Cusack hits another boundary

off' technique very useful and a lot of the guys use it too.

I didn't last too long unfortunately, and patted a soft ball back to Yuvraj for 9. He struck again to get Porty for 75 just after drinks and we eventually were bowled out for 207. With a bit more luck we could have made 240, but we still felt our total was competitive.

When India started their innings I was standing at second slip, with

PAIR OF LEGENDS: *One of the most destructive batsmen in the history of the game... and Sachin Tendulkar! Paul Stirling gets to meet one of his heroes*

Stirlo at first. Boyd ran in and bowled an excellent delivery to Sehwag, but he went for it and it rocketed it to the ropes. I just looked across at Niall and exchanged a worried glance.

Boyd had been getting a bit of stick and there was even speculation that he might be rested, but I'd always back the big man. He bowled beautifully against India – 10 overs for 34 is seriously tight bowling at this level, especially when Sehwag cracked two fours off the first three balls. I love the way Sehwag bats, he's completely carefree. It's a great way to play cricket and it's great to watch, but not from second slip.

TJ came on next and he'd been asking us all week whether he should bring back the chicken dance that he had made famous in 2007. It was amazing to see him doing that stupid strut after his first ball of the day when Sehwag chipped a leading edge back to him. When he picked up Gautan Gambhir two overs later we had them 24 for 2, but he slipped in his follow through and banged down hard on his knee after bowling just five overs and had to go off.

That was a huge blow to us, as TJ has been a huge part of all our great wins over the past decade. He spent the rest of the game in the hospital.

George came on and bowled brilliantly to a man twice his age. Sachin Tendulkar, the greatest batsman of the last 20 years, had scored the first of his six World Cup centuries before Dockers was even born.

He bowled him a good, flighted first ball but Sachin creamed it to the boundary. 'That's a bit rough' I thought, but I knew Dockers wouldn't be affected by anything. He lets everything go over his head.

In all he bowled 12 balls to Tendulkar, who scored three more singles, before he tossed one a little higher and the little guy missed it and was given out, plumb LBW. George loves learning new things and works very

THE CHICKEN MAN: *TJ's stupid dance craze has spread all over India*

hard. He has the potential to go a long way.

Tendulkar and Virat Kohli had put on about 60 but we had the two of them back in the dressing room with the score on 100. Dockers had 2-49 and Stirlo 0-45 off their 10 over spells.

The Indian crowd were very quiet but unfortunately we just couldn't separate Dhoni and Yuvraj, who put on 67. I think if we had got Yusuf Pathan in earlier Boyd might have got him out, but the big man had only two overs left. George got Dhoni lbw, but Yusuf finished off that over with 4, 6, 6, and had got his eye in. He finished us off, brutally.

It was good to follow up a great performance against England with another strong, competitive performance. A couple of years ago we probably would have been hockeyed, but everyone played well and we had chances to get a better score with the bat, but we just couldn't kick on.

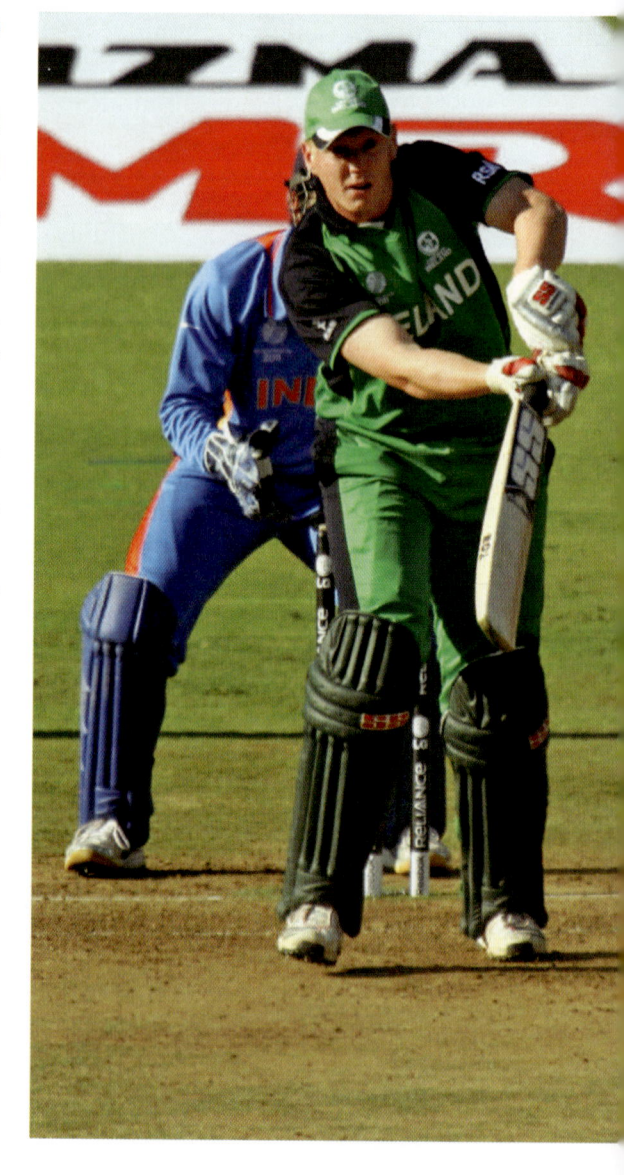

Afterwards Yuvraj gave me his jersey, and he signed it, "to Kevin, great innings v England, best wishes Yuvraj".

INDIA

OOPS: *Early doors for me as I spoon the ball back to Yuvraj*

It was the only jersey I picked up at the World Cup, as I'm not as keen a collector as some of the guys. In 2007 I swapped with Scott Styris of New Zealand and at the twenty20 in England I got Saeed Ajmal of Pakistan. I also swapped with Andrew Flintoff in 2007, and gave that to my Notts team-mate Ryan Sidebottom to get it signed. He still has it in his house!

A SHOCKER: *Gary Wilson seeks clarification from Asoka da Silva about his bizarre dismissal*

CHAPTER 11
IRELAND VERSUS **WEST INDIES**

AS WE GOT READY TO SAY GOODBYE TO BANGALORE – AND many of those who had travelled to support us – all hell broke loose.

My brother Niall was rooming across the corridor but I missed all the drama after the game when he realised his bat bag had gone missing. He was up half the night trying to track them down and was still batless – and very unhappy – when I met him at breakfast.

A truck chartered by the ICC collected all our kit from the stadium and brought it the team hotel, less than a mile away. We all picked up our bags from the lobby but when Niall went down his bag of bats weren't there.

It turned into a major news story for a few days, and Nialler was in a bit of a heap about it. He gets his bats specially made by Gray Nicolls and goes down to their factory in Sussex every year to be measured precisely. One reporter asked him why he couldn't use one of my bats, and he had to explain that I was about eight inches taller than him and bat in a completely different way. He also joked that I use a completely different brand, which mightn't be too amusing to Gray Nicolls.

I'm not that obsessive about my bats, but I wouldn't want anything to happen to them either.

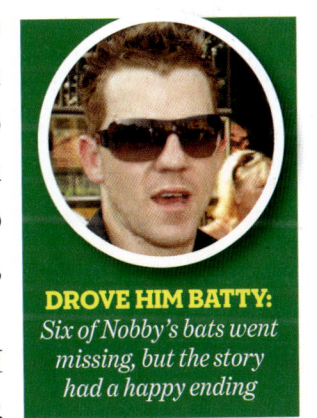

DROVE HIM BATTY: *Six of Nobby's bats went missing, but the story had a happy ending*

My bats are made in India by SS Sunridges so I email them my measurements and requirements, such as big edges. I didn't use the World Cup bat for ages after I got back to Ireland, and will only use it for the big games. I usually go through about five or six bats a year, and when that one ends its days it'll be going up over the mantelpiece!

It all ended happily for Niall, as the bag turned up among the Indian team's gear when they landed in Delhi. He had also been given one by the

Indian batsman Suresh Raina, and his sponsor had flown him out half a dozen more too. He spread the love around the team too, and a few of the guys got a nice new plank.

We had a nice two-hour flight up to Chandigarh, although TJ had a cramped trip with his leg stretched out in a special brace. We were delighted to see the Indian media had given us credit for the night before, with headlines like 'Ireland make India sweat' and 'India survive trial by Ire'.

An editorial in the *Times of India* paid us a lovely tribute: "Ireland have shown throughout the competition that while they may not match the big boys in talent and experience, they possess a steel, spirit and spunk that helps them cope with the most demanding challenges."

Chandigarh was a very nice and well-organised city, but unfortunately we weren't allowed to see very much of it. Being so close to the border with Pakistan, the security there was incredibly tight, with airport scanners for all bags and persons entering the hotel. We were told we would only be allowed leave the hotel with an armed guard, so we only made one outing, to the shops in Sector 17.

Although we were being widely praised, we knew we still had only one win in the bag, and that the game there against West Indies was going to be crucial. The Punjab CA stadium is a 30,000-seater modern structure,

DEVON'S GATE: *I finally claimed the wicket of Devon Smith, but not till he had made 100*

with virtually all seats exposed to the sun, and the few Irish fans that made it there to the suburb of Mohali had a long, hot day. In fact, besides those against the two host nations, there was more support – travelling and local – for Ireland at the games than for any of the opposition teams.

CHARMED LIFE: *An inside edge races away for four*

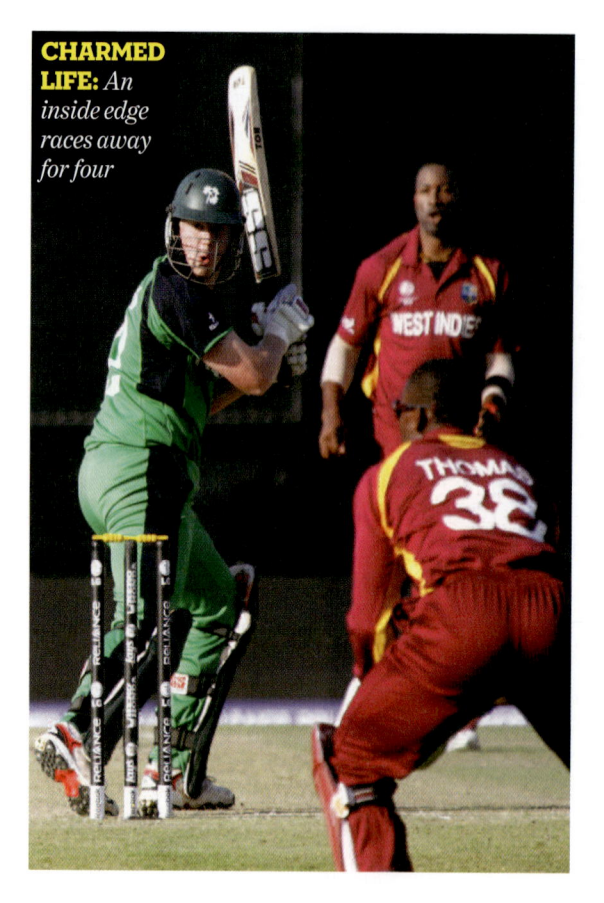

The temperature in Chandigarh was about ten degrees cooler than Bangalore, however, and you could see the foothills of the Himalayas in the distance, less than 100 miles away. With little to divert us, it was good to get involved in some charity initiatives, and Boyd, George and I helped coach a group of pupils from the St Soldier International School. ICC runs a programme to educate schools about the dangers of Aids and HIV so it was good to help out. We ran a little competition and I gave the winning kid one of my Ireland shirts.

I will always remember the West Indies game as a missed opportunity. The key difference between the sides was Kieron Pollard, who we let off the hook a couple of times. We had got a rare boost at the start when Chris Gayle was ruled out with an abdominal strain. He is one of the most destructive batsmen in the world and it was a relief not to have to bowl to him, especially as I was going to have a few more overs than usual in the absence of TJ.

It was a pretty good wicket, but Boyd and Cusy opened with a maiden apiece, and the Windies batted steadily. Shivnarine Chanderpaul and Devon Smith reached 62 off 18 overs when I came on, and Smith picked up my first ball off a length and smacked it back over my head for six.

It was the 25th over before we got our first wicket, when Chanderpaul was caught by Porty at extra cover, and then I bowled Darren Bravo in the same over. Dockers came on and got Sarwan, which brought Kieron Pollard to the middle.

Pollard is another monster batsman who can destroy a team, and our plan was to keep the spinners away from him. Our plan was for the seamers to bowl back of a length to him, with the odd bouncer and slower ball bouncer.

I came on for the first over of the powerplay and didn't get my length right: and he put two balls out of ground. In the same over we had a chance

SAWN OFF: *I'm convinced Gary Wilson would have made a century*

to run him out, but John Boy had just one stump to aim at and the big man escaped. He got away with it again in the next over, bowled by André. He tried to flick the ball over square leg and got a leading edge. Willo ran around and dived forward, but wasn't able to hang on.

Smith made a gritty hundred which was important for the West Indies, but Pollard's innings was the difference between the teams. He made his 50 off 35 balls – just five slower than mine against England – and there was a chance he might take my fastest hundred record away from me.

I came back and got two more wickets in an over, Smith and Darren Sammy, but Pollard ruined my bowling figures with 2, 4, 6, 6, 1, off my ninth over. I was more than relieved when he was caught by Boyd at long-off next over for 94 off 55 balls.

KIERON POLLARD: *Ruined my bowling figures with 19 runs off a single over*

We bowled them out for 275 – my 4-71 was a personal best in ODIs, despite Pollard – and on such a good wicket we were still confident that we could chase the target.

The Windies opened the bowling with the tall spinner Suleiman Benn, and Stirlo was out caught bat and pad in his first over. Joycey came in then and hit two beautiful drives that raced away for four. Ed is a world class batsman and I think he was a bit disappointed that he hadn't got a big score yet in the competition.

He was magnificent that day, counter-attacking against the speedy Kemar Roach. He and Willo put on 91 to bring us to 177 for 3, needing seven-and-a-half off the last 13 overs. Sadly, with a century for the taking, Joycey played round a good ball from André Russell and was out for 84.

I came in watched Gary get his fifty, but I scooped a ball from Sammy too high over long on and Pollard came diving in to catch it.

We still had a great chance when one of the most controversial decisions of the World Cup destroyed our hopes. Willo was given out LBW by the

ED JOYCE: *Brilliant innings in Mohali*

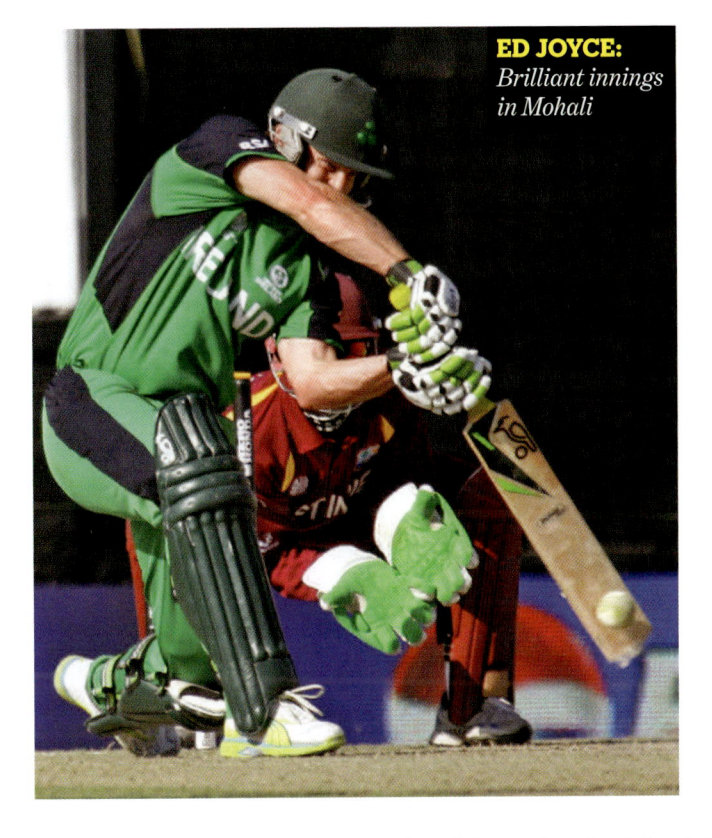

Sri Lankan umpire Asoka de Silva, and immediately called for a review of the decision. De Silva asked the TV umpire Bruce Oxenford on his walkie-talkie 'Did it hit his pad or bat first?' The big screen showed he had been hit outside the line of off stump, so we relaxed – but then de Silva put his finger in the air again. Willo was a bit upset by this and asked for him to look at it again but then the umpire said he wasn't playing a shot.

We couldn't understand what was going on. Porty asked "Surely if you are asking if it was pad first or bat first, you know he is playing a shot?"

We fell away badly after that, and were all out for 227, despite Dockers clattering a few nice fours.

The dressing room afterwards was livid. Simmo was walking around raging at anyone that would listen, and poor Willo was screaming in the showers, still in his full gear and pads.

I'm still convinced that Willo would have got 100 not out, as the Windies just had no answer to him. Every ball was coming off the middle of the bat. I just sat there shaking my head. I knew that, barring a miracle, our World Cup was over.

HORSES FOR COURSES:
Ruth-Ann and I had a memorable day at the races in Kolkata

CHAPTER 12
IRELAND VERSUS SOUTH AFRICA

THERE WAS STILL A BIT OF CHUNTERING AMONG THE GUYS AS we flew out of Chandigarh, but there was nothing to be done now but continue to play well and, hopefully, pick up a couple more wins. Even then we probably needed someone else to do us a favour, but the one thing we could be proud of was that we made Group B a highly competitive contest – which removed one of the gripes of the anti-associates brigade. Group A was a poor competition, with Zimbabwe, Kenya and Canada never looking like they would even challenge a full member, let alone beat one, and that group was over ten days early.

Although Kolkata was only two hours away by air, for some reason we had to fly down to Mumbai and then on – which meant two flights of two hours.

We were billeted again in one of the Taj hotels, which were very comfortable. Sadly, we were warned that we couldn't leave the hotel without an escort and that was made into a big deal. Nialler is big into tiger conservation and as we were in the capital of West Bengal he was looking forward to visiting the zoo, especially as it was just across the road! But sadly the police officers just wouldn't let him.

Roy Torrens eventually approached an ICC official and politely told him that we were staying in a prison. A very nice and comfortable one, but a prison just the same. Things improved after that!

We were still confident playing South Africa, who had just lost to England. They had a good bowling attack but their batting wasn't nearly as strong as India's so we felt we could keep their total down.

It was fantastic to play in a ground like Eden Gardens, one of the most famous cricket stadiums in the world. I remember seeing videos of a famous World Cup final there between Australia and England, and they used to pack 130,000 in here for a Test match. The stadium has been rebuilt and its capacity is now down to a mere 70,000!

The climate in Kolkata is very hard to deal with if you're playing an active sport. The humidity is ridiculous – it was 91% on the day of the game – and your clothes become drenched quite quickly. We usually warm up for practice or a game with 15 minutes of touch rugby, but that became almost impossible in Eden Gardens.

We won the toss and stuck them in, and welcomed TJ back to the team. He came in for André, who had picked up a serious bug in Mohali which stayed with him for all the time we spent in Kolkata. He was so dehydrated at one stage that he had to go to hospital and spent a couple of days in a nursing home afterwards. He was gutted to have to miss the game against the country he was born in.

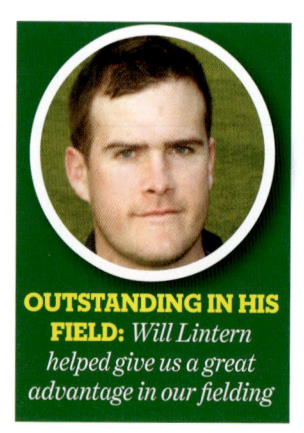

South Africa started cautiously but just as Hashim Amla started to play his shots he carted the ball to Dockers at third-man who held a brilliant catch. The new man, Morne van Wyk, drilled a ball straight at me next over at short cover but, although I got both hands to it, I just couldn't hold on. TJ was not happy – and he's not a good guy to drop a catch off.

OUTSTANDING IN HIS FIELD: *Will Lintern helped give us a great advantage in our fielding*

Our fielding was generally top class though, and we got a chance to show off here. With the score on 52-1, John Mooney, at midwicket, spotted Graeme Smith had backed up too far and with a lightning pick-up and throw he ran their skipper out by inches.

Their dangerman Jacques Kallis was starting to hit fours when JP Duminy hit the ball out to cover where Porty was prowling. He picked up on the run, threw as he fell and the ball went straight to Nialler's gloves where he thrashed Kallis's stumps. Porty was literally parallel to the ground when he threw which is amazingly hard to do.

SOUTH AFRICA

I have to give a lot of credit to Will Lintern, the fielding coach who has been on board since April 2010. Will is an English guy who comes over every now and again to teach us fielding techniques based on his experience of baseball in the United States.

One of the things he showed us is how we can get a quicker and more accurate throw by having your feet point towards the target. He would train us by first getting us to pick up a stationary ball, rotate our feet, and throw to the target. We would then move onto a moving ball, and the speed would increase. His main point was the quicker you get your feet into position the better the throw.

At the start of the winter Will came over to work on our arm strength, and gave us exercises and drills to work on from all distances and angles for 18 minutes every day.

If you ask anyone around the world of cricket about Ireland, one of the first things they'll mention is our fielding. This goes right back to the Adi Birrell era when he told us that, although we mightn't be able to bowl as fast as other teams, or hit the ball as hard, we can certainly outfield anyone – and we did that in both 2007 and 2011.

It was an area we really scored in: ten of our 60 wickets at the competition came from run outs, including a world record four in four balls against Holland. On the last ball of the innings against the Dutch John Boy threw in from 85 metres away and the ball went straight into Niall's gloves.

The run-outs had the South Africans rattled, and it was soon 117 for 5 when TJ snapped up a sharp catch at slip to dismiss Faf du Plessis. But we couldn't press the advantage from there. Colin Ingram and Duminy batted well until the 40th over when they passed 200. Duminy was batting really well and accelerated as the overs ran out. He was all set for a hundred when he tried to hit John Boy down the ground in the last over. He got under the ball and I ran around, dived and came up with the ball in my hand!

BAILING OUT: *Porty and Nialler rush to congratulate Dockers, who has just bowled Morne Van Wyk for 42*

Their total of 272 was a big one, and they had a pretty fabulous bowling attack to defend it. They had bowled England out for 171, Holland 120 and Bangladesh 78, so we knew it would be difficult. Their bowlers – Dale Steyn, Morne Morkel, Jacques Kallis and the three quality spinners – were probably the best at the tournament, and at that stage they were joint-favourites with India.

We were pretty hockeyed to be honest; it was our worst batting performance since Bangladesh.

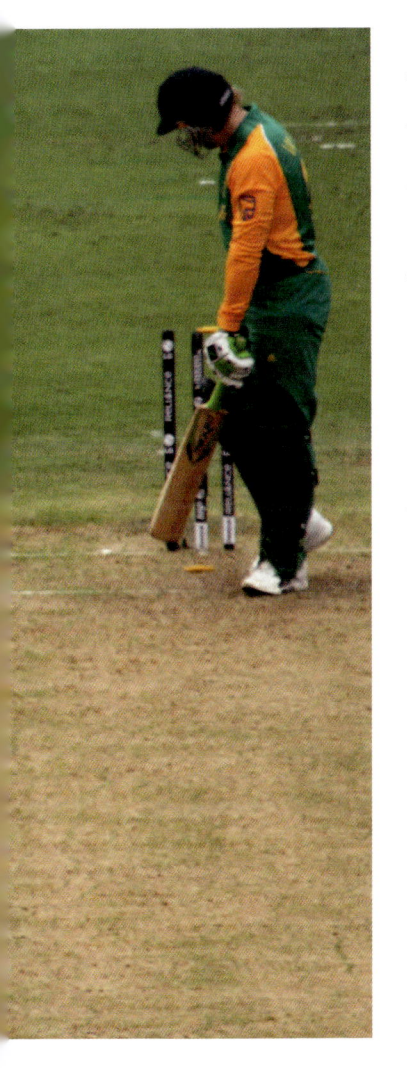

Nialler cracked a huge six off Morne Morkel but then nicked one off Kallis. We struggled to build any sort of partnership, though Gary Wilson continued to hit the ball well. We were all out for 141, our lowest score in a one-day game for almost three years.

We met a few of the South African guys in the hotel afterwards, and there was a lot of interest in Graeme Smith's new girlfriend – Morgan Deane from Cork, who is one of Jedward's backing singers. Nialler knows Morgan from Dublin and offered to give her an Ireland jersey for the game!

Graeme and Morgan were very sociable in the bar chatting away with our supporters, most of whom worked in Kolkata at various development and charity projects. He said he was planning a golf trip to Ireland so Big Roy invited them to sample some of his famous hospitality at his Port Hotel in Portrush. Good luck to him!

After saying goodnight to one famous pop singer, I went upstairs to find I had received an email from another – Roger Whelan of The Roj Light, Railway Union and Ireland. He attached a link to a YouTube video which made me grin when the page opened – a song called *'Kevin O'Brien'*!

Roj told me had inspired by the England game and just sat down and wrote the song. It was very catchy and I had to try hard to make sure I didn't sing it in front of any of the guys! I watched it a few times after I got home and it brought a tear to my eye. I hope Roj doesn't mind if I print his lyrics here:

"KEVIN O'BRIEN"
By Roger Whelan/The RojLight

In the heat of an Indian night
A broken nation breathes new life
Standing tall against the British might
The winds of change are in sight

Now's our time to shine...

Kevin O'Brien
Yeah he destroyed the English tonight
Lifting Irish hearts and minds
Yeah cos history is made in the sky

And it'll never be the same
When you believe you can do anything
And John Boy's will to be brave
Go right ahead and beat them at their own game!

The Emperor falls from up on high
I guess we always knew why
An imperial power and a lost empire
The old Eire on the funeral pyre

Now's our time to shine...

Kevin O'Brien
Yeah he destroyed the English tonight
Lifting Irish hearts and minds
Yeah cos history is made in the sky

And it'll never be the same
When you believe you can do anything
And John Boy's will to be brave
Go right ahead and beat them at their own game!

BIG HANDS: *Trent Johnston catches Faf du Plessis at slip off Stirlo*

Roj won three caps for Ireland in 2007, and took three prize scalps – Sachin Tendulkar, AB de Villiers and Ravi Bopara. He retired from all cricket at the end of that summer, aged 27, to concentrate on singing with his punk band The Stimulants. Nialler was actually a founder member of The Stimulants; he thinks he has a good voice.

They wouldn't let me join the band, but I came along to one of their practices with this lyric called 'Playground Blues'. They were really impressed. Unfortunately their English teacher opened the poetry book at that page a few weeks later and I was rumbled – I had nicked it from a poem by Adrian Mitchell!

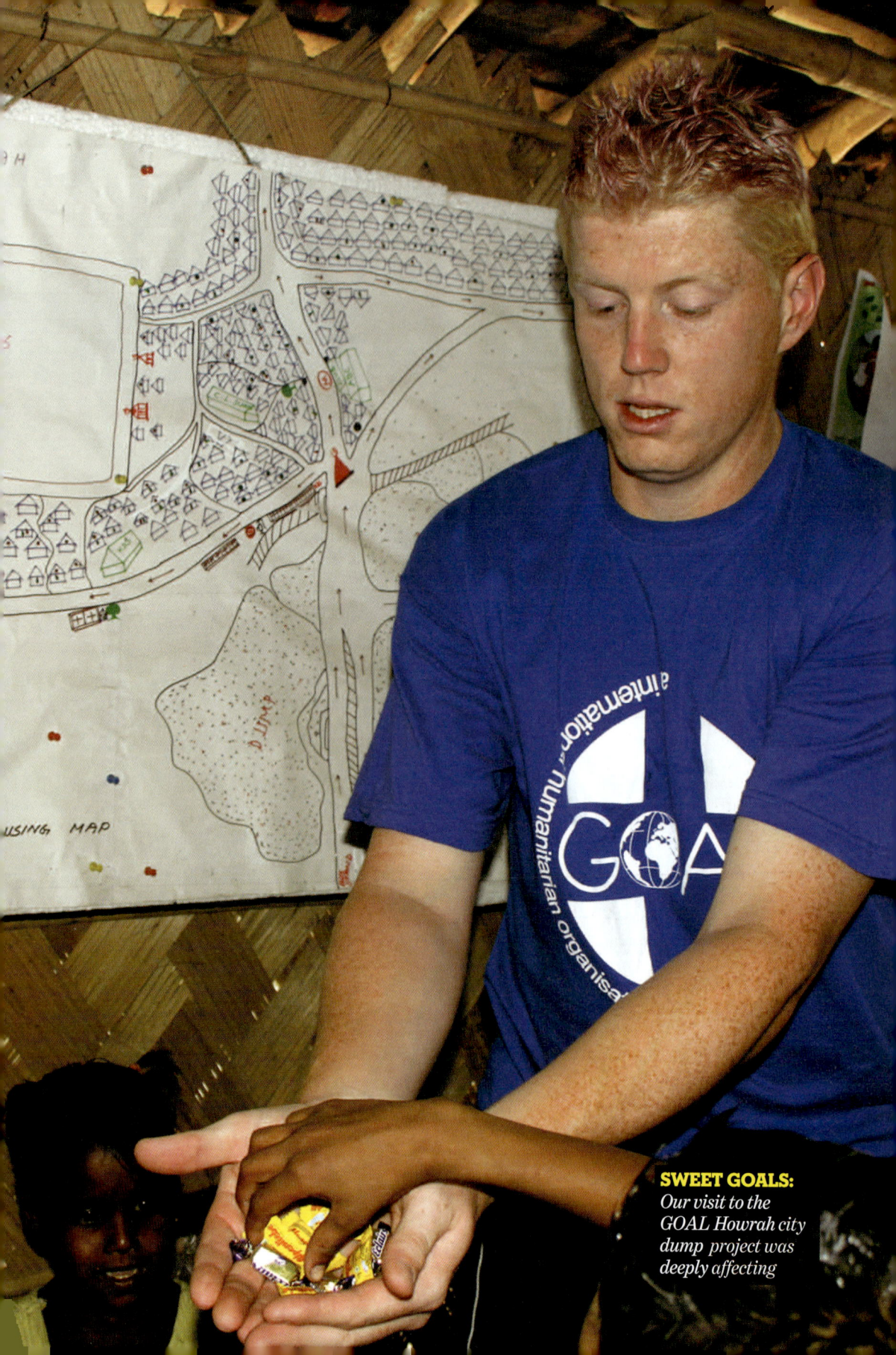

SWEET GOALS: *Our visit to the GOAL Howrah city dump project was deeply affecting*

CHAPTER 13
IRELAND VERSUS HOLLAND

KOLKATA, OR CALCUTTA AS IT USED TO BE KNOWN, HAS A BIT of a bad reputation. Besides cricket, all we had ever heard of it was that Mother Teresa had her home there and that John O'Shea's GOAL charity raised funds to help the street children there. I had rattled a few buckets for GOAL in my time at Star of the Sea.

When we were in Bangalore I got a call from John asking would I like to be a GOAL ambassador. I was enormously honoured to follow such sporting greats as John McEnroe and Brian O'Driscoll, and delighted to help in any way.

I met an Irish architect, Ciaran Mac Mathúna, who told me how he works in Kolkata helping to install toilets in schools, which will help reduce illness and therefore absenteeism. But there are 60,000 schools in this city of 15 million citizens, so it is an impossible job.

He took Alex, Ed and I to the Howrah City dump on the outskirts of Kolkata. Seeing the poverty people live in while we were driving through the streets to get there was bad enough, but when we arrived it was unbelievable. We were brought in jeeps through the mountains of rubbish discarded by the people of Kolkata to this village where 600 people scrape a living from scavenging rags, plastic and metal. The stench was unbearable and it became a bit overwhelming for all the senses.

The idea of people living in a dump was distressing to us, but it was astonishing at how happy the people were. People in Ireland don't know how lucky they are. They mightn't have as much money as they used to have, but when you see how these people live you are very grateful.

We went to a tiny, baking hot school which was little more than a shack and about the size of our dressing room back in Railway. Sixty kids aged up to six were crammed into the single, steaming room. The children were

LITTLE & LARGE: There's 22 inches difference between the height of this pair!

great fun and obviously don't know any different. They sang a few songs for us and Roy did a little song and dance routine too. We handed out a few sweeties and had a chat with the teachers who told us how GOAL has been pumping money in to help their facilities. Outside the door was an open sewer and around the corner was a disgusting, diseased lake where a toddler drowned earlier this year.

There is one television in Bhagar Colony and they all told me how they had watched me bat against England – I think the pink-top haircut was a great success with the Indians!

We were glad to be able to use our celebrity to help raise awareness of the great work that Irish charities are doing in India, and we also visited projects run by SUAS and the Hope Foundation. Nialler was invited to a St Patrick's Day party by SUAS and had a great time there. He met up with a distinguished family of Indians called the O'Briens! The father, Neil O'Brien, was the first man to bring quiz shows to Indian TV

THE O'BRIENS TURN UP EVERYWHERE: *Neil O'Brien and Nialler discuss the Bengal side of the family at the SUAS reception*

and became a huge celebrity there and later an MP. His son Derek is the top quizmaster in India and also a minister in West Bengal. Niall said they were a lovely bunch and they sent me a present of their latest quiz book.

John Boy's mother, Frances, also paid a visit to a SUAS school project where she and Yvonne Botha got chatting to a group of mothers. They told them that they each saved 20 rupees (35 cent) a week towards buying a sewing machine. Frances came back to the hotel and organised a whip around of all the squad and supporters and she raised enough to buy them a new sewing machine straight away, which was a fantastic thing to do.

We got one more chance to escape from the Taj before we left Kolkata – a day at the races! We were invited to attend the Royal Calcutta Turf Club as VIP guests. It was a beautiful racecourse, situated right smack in the middle of the city with lovely views of the fine old buildings. We had a very enjoyable day with plenty of nice food and drink and all our party was invited, including the reporters and the last of the supporters, which was our former PRO Peter Breen, who now works for Leinster Rugby.

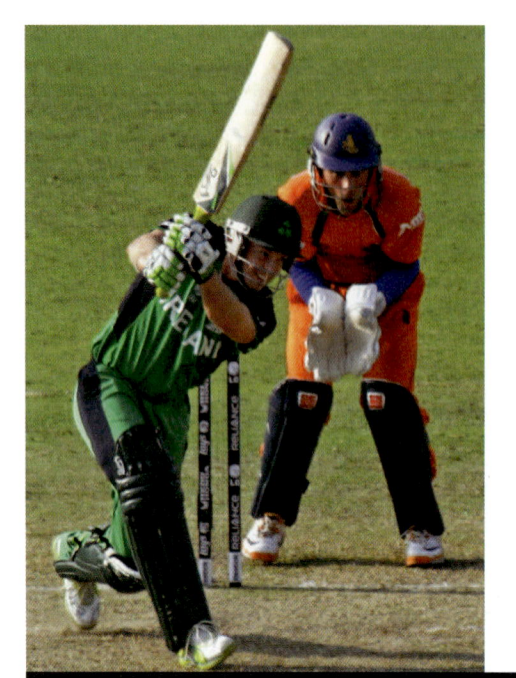

DUTCH TREAT: *Ed Joyce (left) and Paul Stirling put the Netherlands bowling to the sword*

The Royal Calcutta very kindly renamed their feature race The Ireland Trophy and asked Porty, Trent and I to present the trophy to the winning trainer, Bharat Singh. The jockeys were tiny, and when the winner, Shailesh Shinde, came up to collect his prize from TJ the spectators roared laughing. Barry Chambers set up a great photo with Boydo (6 feet 8 inches) and Shailesh (4 feet 10 inches).

We had the whole VIP balcony to ourselves, and the wives and girlfriends had great fun dressing up to the nines and getting plenty of attention. The tote runners were very well informed and almost everyone ended up in the black – myself and Nialler brought home about 5,000 rupees, which is about €80. The funniest episode was when this Indian man met Joycey and Boyd and kept calling them 'Kevin and Niall'. When TJ finally put him right he said "thank you Mr Mooney"!

It was great to relax, but we got our heads down the next morning to prepare for what was, in some ways, the most important game of the tournament for us. It would have been terrible to lose to Holland because it would have left people thinking the win over England was a one-off. We also didn't want anyone to think that Holland were close to us in playing standards – they haven't beaten us since 2007 and we believe we are way ahead of them. The pressures were different for us too, because people expected us to hammer Holland, which we knew wouldn't be easy, especially if their star Ryan ten Doeschate clicked.

And click he did. TenDo had a fantastic tournament, which he ended as the only man to score two centuries.

We picked up two of their best batters, Tom Cooper and Alex Kervezee, quite cheaply, but ten Doeschate was in dangerous mood. He made 106, and captain Peter Borren chipped in with 84, before that hilarious last over when we ran four of them out off the last four balls I bowled. We weren't too happy to concede over 300, and were a bit rattled that George had to go off to hospital with a dislocated shoulder that kept him out of cricket for two months.

STIRLING MESS: *Kieran O'Reilly treats Paul for severe cramp after his innings in Kolkata*

But we knew that we were one of only three countries to ever successfully chase down 300 in a World Cup match – and we knew we could do it again. Porty and Stirlo hadn't really got off to a good start in any game so far – 23 was their biggest partnership – but they certainly cashed in this time. We knew the wicket was good and that Stirlo was never going to go through a whole tournament without making a big score.

Stirlo was unbelievable. We always knew what he was capable of, but that day he showed the world as he became the youngest ever century-maker in a World Cup, beating the great Ricky Ponting. He and Porty batted aggressively and completely knocked the Dutch off their lines and lengths. Stirlo reached his fifty in 25 balls – five balls faster than my two-week-old Irish record!

They put on 177 for the first wicket, which fell in only the 27th over so we were cruising. Porty made 68 and Paul 101 off 73 balls – which meant Ireland had the fastest and third-fastest World Cup centuries in our locker.

Ed, Nialler and Willo kept up the pressure and Nobby made a well-deserved fifty, his third in World Cups. He showed me the career World Cup records on the Cricket Europe website after the game and he's Ireland's top-scorer with 421 runs – and I'm next with 368.

I came out with 30 needed and just watched as Nialler played some great shots and raced past fifty. We needed 14 off the last three overs but

THE END OF THE ADVENTURE: *Billy Doctrove signals six as Niall and I finish off the Dutch*

I wanted to finish it early and dumped Pieter Seelar back over his head for two sixes, my 94th and 95th for Ireland (which is 93 more than my dad scored!). And with that I put my bat under my arm and walked off with Niall, happy at a job well done.

I arrived in the dressing room to a remarkable sight: Brendan Connor holding Stirlo's legs vertically up in the air. The big man was in total agony as his legs had seized up with cramp. He couldn't even walk out to collect his Man of the Match award. There was a bit of sympathy for Stirlo, but a fair few sniggers too!

AFTERWORD

HOME WE FLEW FROM THE WORLD CUP, WITH A FEW REGRETS that we hadn't been able to make the quarter-finals. The defeat in Bangladesh still rankled, and the way we lost to the West Indies. With a bit of luck we would have finished third in the group and traveled to Colombo to face Sri Lanka. Instead we flew from Kolkata to Dubai to London and home to Dublin, where RSA hosted a fantastic welcome party. The celebrations continued that night in Krystle nightclub, where it was great to link up with Rangan and all our Irish pals.

KRYSTLE PALACE: *Club-mate Rangan Arulchelvan threw a great party for the team*

I had a few weeks off, and organised an Easter Camp for youngsters in Railway which I really enjoyed. I had a couple of games for the club, helping them to beat our Sandymount rivals Pembroke, before I flew to Bristol to join Gloucestershire. It was great to be back in professional cricket again, testing myself against the best players and playing alongside such greats as Muttiah Muralitharan and Hamish Marshall.

I got to meet a few of the Irish guys around the circuit – although I don't think Paul Stirling was too happy when we met up at the end of June at Uxbridge! We played Middlesex in a T20 game and Hamish and I broke the world record first wicket partnership, and the team set the highest total ever made in England. I made 100 in 44 balls – faster than Bangalore – and Hamish got a ton too. It was nice to be back breaking batting records!

I still get flashbacks to that amazing night in Bangalore, and it still prickles the back of my neck when I think of some of those shots and the feeling we had as a team to beat England. It was annoying that ICC tried to cut us out of the next World Cup, but our CEO Warren Deutrom won that battle. Ireland has a fantastic bunch of players and we really worked hard to show the world how good we are, and to give the people back home something to smile about. I hope you agree that we succeeded in that.

SCORECARDS

BANGLADESH V IRELAND
Shere Bangla National Stadium, Mirpur   25 February 2011 - day/night

Bangladesh			M	B	4s	6s	SR
Tamim Iqbal	c Porterfield b Botha	**44**	52	43	7	0	102.32
Imrul Kayes	st †N O'Brien b Mooney	**12**	29	12	2	0	100.00
Junaid Siddique	run out (Joyce)	**3**	9	8	0	0	37.50
Mushfiqur Rahim†	c White b Dockrell	**36**	95	66	2	0	54.54
Shakib Al Hasan*	c & b Botha	**16**	17	20	3	0	80.00
Raqibul Hasan	run out (White)	**38**	87	69	1	0	55.07
Mohammad Ashraful	c White b Dockrell	**1**	9	6	0	0	16.66
Naeem Islam	c Dockrell b Johnston	**29**	64	38	3	0	76.31
Shafiul Islam	lbw b Botha	**2**	14	17	0	0	11.76
Abdur Razzak	b Johnston	**11**	28	16	0	0	68.75
Rubel Hossain	not out	**1**	7	2	0	0	100.00
Extras	(b 2, w 8, nb 1)	**11**					
Total	(all out; 49.2 overs)	**205**	(4.15 runs per over)				

Fall: 1-53 (Imrul Kayes, 6.3 ov), 2-61 (Junaid Siddique, 8.5 ov), 3-68 (Tamim Iqbal, 11.1 ov),4-86 (Shakib , 15.2 ov), 5-147 (Mushfiqur Rahim, 33.3 ov), 6-151 (Mohammad Ashraful, 35.2 ov),7-159 (Raqibul, 38.1 ov), 8-170 (Shafiul, 42.3 ov), 9-193 (Abdur Razzak, 47.6 ov), 10-205 (Naeem Islam, 49.2 ov)

	O	M	R	W	Econ	
WB Rankin	9	0	62	0	6.88	(4w)
DT Johnston	8.2	0	40	**2**	4.80	(1nb)
JF Mooney	7	0	25	**1**	3.57	(1w)
AC Botha	9	1	32	**3**	3.55	(1w)
GH Dockrell	10	2	23	**2**	2.30	
PR Stirling	4	0	13	0	3.25	
KJ O'Brien	**2**	**0**	**8**	**0**	**4.00**	

Ireland (target: 206 from 50 overs)		R	M	B	4s	6s	SR
WTS Porterfield*	c Raqibul b Shakib	**20**	31	30	2	0	66.66
PR Stirling	st †Mushfiqur b Razzak	**9**	18	10	1	0	90.00
EC Joyce	c & b Mohammad Ashraful	**16**	45	35	0	0	45.71
NJ O'Brien†	c Tamim b Shakib	**38**	64	52	3	0	73.07
AR White	b Mohammad Ashraful	**10**	20	27	1	0	37.03
KJ O'Brien	**c sub (Shuvo) b Shafiul**	**37**	**46**	**40**	**3**	**1**	**92.50**
AC Botha	b Shafiul	**22**	55	36	2	0	61.11
JF Mooney	b Naeem Islam	**0**	16	8	0	0	0.00
DT Johnston	lbw b Shafiul	**6**	10	6	1	0	100.00
GH Dockrell	not out	**4**	21	12	0	0	33.33
WB Rankin	c Junaid b Shafiul	**3**	12	13	0	0	23.07
Extras	(lb 9, w 4)	**13**					
Total	(all out; 45 overs)	**178**	(3.95 runs per over)				

Fall: 1-23 (Stirling, 5.3 ov), 2-36 (Porterfield, 9.1 ov), 3-75 (Joyce, 18.1 ov), 4-93 (White, 24.4 ov),5-110 (N O'Brien, 27.4 ov), 6-151 (K O'Brien, 36.4 ov), 7-164 (Mooney, 39.4 ov), 8-168 (Botha, 40.1 ov),9-171 (Johnston, 42.1 ov), 10-178 (Rankin, 44.6 ov)

	O	M	R	W	Econ	
Shafiul Islam	8	1	21	**4**	2.62	(2w)
Abdur Razzak	8	0	30	**1**	3.75	
Naeem Islam	9	1	36	**1**	4.00	
Shakib Al Hasan	8	0	28	**2**	3.50	(1w)
Mohammad Ashraful	9	0	42	**2**	4.66	(1w)
Rubel Hossain	3	0	12	0	4.00	

Toss: Bangladesh, who chose to bat
Umpires: Aleem Dar (Pakistan) and RJ Tucker (Australia)
Match referee: RS Mahanama (Sri Lanka)
Bangladesh won by 27 runs

Attendance: 26,728
TV umpire: BF Bowden (New Zealand)
Reserve umpire: M Erasmus (South Africa)
Player of the match: Tamim Iqbal (Bangladesh)

ENGLAND V IRELAND

M Chinnaswamy Stadium, Bangalore 2 March 2011 (day/night)

England		R	M	B	4s	6s	SR
AJ Strauss*	b Dockrell	34	61	37	2	1	91.89
KP Pietersen	c †NJ O'Brien b Stirling	59	77	50	7	2	118.00
IJL Trott	b Mooney	92	126	92	9	0	100.00
IR Bell	c Stirling b Mooney	81	102	86	6	1	94.18
PD Collingw'd	c **K O'Brien** b Mooney	16	21	11	0	1	145.45
MJ Prior†	b Johnston	6	7	5	1	0	120.00
TT Bresnan	c Johnston b Mooney	4	23	8	0	0	50.00
MH Yardy	b Johnston	3	8	6	0	0	50.00
GP Swann	not out	9	8	5	1	0	180.00
Extras	(b 1, lb 2, w 20)	23					
Total	(8 wkts; 50 overs; 220 mins)	327	(6.54 runs per over)				

Did not bat: SCJ Broad, JM Anderson

Fall: 1-91 (Strauss, 13.3 ov), 2-111 (Pietersen, 16.6 ov), 3-278 (Bell, 42.6 ov), 4-288 (Trott, 44.3 ov), 5-299 (Prior, 45.6 ov), 6-312 (Collingwood, 46.6 ov), 7-317 (Yardy, 48.3 ov), 8-327 (Bresnan, 49.6 ov)

	O	M	R	W	Econ	
WB Rankin	7	0	51	0	7.28	(4w)
DT Johnston	10	0	58	2	5.80	
AR Cusack	4	0	39	0	9.75	(1w)
GH Dockrell	10	0	68	1	6.80	(5w)
JF Mooney	9	0	63	4	7.00	(1w)
PR Stirling	10	0	45	1	4.50	

Ireland (target: 328 from 50 overs)		R	M	B	4s	6s	SR
WTS Porterfield*	b Anderson	0	1	1	0	0	0.00
PR Stirling	c Pietersen b Bresnan	32	45	28	5	1	114.28
EC Joyce	st †Prior b Swann	32	90	61	3	0	52.45
NJ O'Brien†	b Swann	29	37	36	2	1	80.55
GC Wilson	lbw b Swann	3	17	14	0	0	21.42
KJ O'Brien	**run out (†Prior/Bresnan)**	**113**	**123**	**63**	**13**	**6**	**179.36**
AR Cusack	run out (Broad/Collingwood)	47	80	58	3	1	81.03
JF Mooney	not out	33	40	30	6	0	110.00
DT Johnston	not out	7	6	4	1	0	175.00
Extras	(b 5, lb 16, w 12)	33					
Total	(7 wkts; 49.1 overs; 223 mins)	329	(6.69 runs per over)				

Did not bat: GH Dockrell, WB Rankin

Fall: 1-0 (Porterfield, 0.1 ov), 2-62 (Stirling, 9.5 ov), 3-103 (N O'Brien, 20.2 ov), 4-106 (Joyce, 22.2 ov), 5-111 (Wilson, 24.2 ov), 6-273 (Cusack, 41.3 ov), 7-317 (K O'Brien, 48.1 ov)

	O	M	R	W	Econ	
JM Anderson	8.1	1	49	1	6.00	(1w)
SCJ Broad	9	0	73	0	8.11	(2w)
TT Bresnan	10	0	64	1	6.40	(2w)
MH Yardy	7	0	49	0	7.00	(2w)
GP Swann	10	0	47	3	4.70	
PD Collingwood	5	0	26	0	5.20	

Toss: England, who chose to bat
Umpires: Aleem Dar (Pakistan) and BF Bowden (New Zealand)
Match referee: RS Mahanama (Sri Lanka)
Ireland won by 3 wickets (with 5 balls remaining)

Attendance: 23,500
TV umpire: M Erasmus (South Africa)
Reserve umpire: RJ Tucker (Australia)
Player of the match KJ O'Brien (Ireland)

SCORECARDS

INDIA V IRELAND

M Chinnaswamy Stadium, Bangalore   6 March 2011 (day/night)

Ireland		R	M	B	4s	6s	SR
WTS Porterfield*	c Harbhajan b Yuvraj	75	146	104	6	1	72.11
PR Stirling	b Khan	0	2	1	0	0	0.00
EC Joyce	c †Dhoni b Khan	4	8	5	1	0	80.00
NJ O'Brien†	run out (Kohli/†Dhoni)	46	93	78	3	0	58.97
AR White	c †Dhoni b Yuvraj	5	8	10	0	0	50.00
KJ O'Brien	**c & b Yuvraj**	**9**	**14**	**13**	**1**	**0**	**69.23**
AR Cusack	lbw b Yuvraj	24	49	30	3	0	80.00
JF Mooney	lbw b Yuvraj	5	19	17	0	0	29.41
DT Johnston	lbw b Patel	17	38	20	2	0	85.00
GH Dockrell	c †Dhoni b Khan	3	19	10	0	0	30.00
WB Rankin	not out	1	5	1	0	0	100.00
Extras	(lb 4, w 8, nb 6)	18					
Total	(all out; 47.5 ovs; 205 mins)	207	(4.32 runs per over)				

Fall: 1-1 (Stirling, 0.4 ov), 2-9 (Joyce, 2.3 ov), 3-122 (NJ O'Brien, 26.5 ov), 4-129 (White, 29.1 ov), 5-147 (KJ O'Brien, 33.4 ov), 6-160 (Porterfield, 37.1 ov), 7-178 (Mooney, 41.5 ov), 8-184 (Cusack, 43.4 ov), 9-201 (Dockrell, 46.6 ov), 10-207 (Johnston, 47.5 ov)

	O	M	R	W	Econ	
Z Khan	9	1	30	**3**	3.33	(1w)
MM Patel	4.5	0	25	**1**	5.17	(1w)
YK Pathan	7	1	32	0	4.57	
Harbhajan Singh	9	1	29	0	3.22	(1w)
PP Chawla	8	0	56	0	7.00	(2nb, 3w)
Yuvraj Singh	10	0	31	**5**	3.10	(1w)

India (target: 208 runs from 50 overs)		R	M	B	4s	6s	SR
V Sehwag	c & b Johnston	5	5	3	1	0	166.66
SR Tendulkar	lbw b Dockrell	38	91	56	4	0	67.85
G Gambhir	c Cusack b Johnston	10	18	15	2	0	66.66
V Kohli	run out (Dockrell/**K O'Brien**)	34	82	53	3	0	64.15
Yuvraj Singh	not out	50	108	75	3	0	66.66
MS Dhoni*†	lbw b Dockrell	34	68	50	2	0	68.00
YK Pathan	not out	30	23	24	2	3	125.00
Extras	(lb 4, w 5)	9					
Total	(5 wkts; 46 overs; 200 mins)	210	(4.56 runs per over)				

Did not bat: Harbhajan Singh, PP Chawla, Z Khan, MM Patel

Fall: 1-9 (Sehwag, 1.1 ov), 2-24 (Gambhir, 5.2 ov), 3-87 (Tendulkar, 20.1 ov), 4-100 (Kohli, 23.4 ov), 5-167 (Dhoni, 40.1 ov)

	O	M	R	W	Econ	
WB Rankin	10	1	34	0	3.40	(2w)
DT Johnston	5	1	16	**2**	3.20	(1w)
GH Dockrell	10	0	49	**2**	4.90	
JF Mooney	2	0	18	0	9.00	
PR Stirling	10	0	45	0	4.50	(2w)
AR White	5	0	23	0	4.60	
KJ O'Brien	**1**	**0**	**3**	**0**	**3.00**	
AR Cusack	3	0	18	0	6.00	

Toss: India, who chose to field
Umpires: BF Bowden (New Zealand) & RJ Tucker (Australia)
Match referee: RS Mahanama (Sri Lanka)
India won by 5 wickets (with 24 balls remaining)

Attendance: 45,000
TV umpire: M Erasmus (South Africa)
Reserve umpire: Aleem Dar (Pakistan)
Player of the match: Yuvraj Singh (India)

KEVIN O'BRIEN - SIX AFTER SIX

WEST INDIES V IRELAND
Punjab CA Stadium, Mohali, Chandigarh   11 March 2011

West Indies		R	M	B	4s	6s	SR
DS Smith	b **K O'Brien**	**107**	194	133	11	1	80.45
S Chanderpaul	c Porterfield b **K O'Brien**	**35**	102	62	3	0	56.45
DM Bravo	b **K O'Brien**	**0**	2	3	0	0	0.00
RR Sarwan	c Mooney b Dockrell	**10**	29	19	1	0	52.63
KA Pollard	c Rankin b Mooney	**94**	83	55	8	5	170.90
DJG Sammy*	c Dockrell b **K O'Brien**	**4**	1	3	1	0	133.33
DC Thomas†	c †NO'Brien b Rankin	**2**	8	8	0	0	25.00
AD Russell	b Mooney	**3**	15	7	0	0	42.85
NO Miller	not out	**5**	9	6	0	0	83.33
SJ Benn	run out (Botha/Mooney)	**2**	4	2	0	0	100.00
KAJ Roach	c Stirling b Botha	**1**	1	2	0	0	50.00
Extras	(b 3, lb 6, w 3)	**12**					
Total	(all out; 50 overs; 232 mins)	**275**	(5.50 runs per over)				

Fall: 1-89 (Chanderpaul, 24.2 ov), 2-89 (Bravo, 24.5 ov), 3-130 (Sarwan, 31.6 ov), 4-218 (Smith, 42.3 ov), 5-222 (Sammy, 42.6 ov), 6-228 (Thomas, 44.6 ov), 7-267 (Pollard, 48.1 ov), 8-267 (Russell, 48.2 ov), 9-272 (Benn, 49.2 ov), 10-275 (Roach, 49.6 ov)

	O	M	R	W	Econ	
WB Rankin	10	1	35	1	3.50	
AR Cusack	7	1	22	0	3.14	
JF Mooney	9	0	58	2	6.44	(2w)
AC Botha	10	0	56	1	5.60	
KJ O'Brien	**9**	**0**	**71**	**4**	**7.88**	
PR Stirling	2	0	9	0	4.50	
GH Dockrell	3	0	15	1	5.00	(1w)

Ireland (target: 276 from 50 overs)		R	M	B	4s	6s	SR
WTS Porterfield*	c sub (Rampaul) b Sammy	**11**	52	34	2	0	32.35
PR Stirling	c Sammy b Benn	**5**	7	6	1	0	83.33
EC Joyce	b Russell	**84**	150	106	9	0	79.24
NJ O'Brien†	b Benn	**25**	38	31	2	0	80.64
GC Wilson	lbw b Sammy	**61**	90	62	6	1	98.38
KJ O'Brien	**c Pollard b Sammy**	**5**	**10**	**9**	**0**	**0**	**55.55**
AR Cusack	st †Thomas b Benn	**2**	15	5	0	0	40.00
JF Mooney	b Roach	**6**	18	7	1	0	85.71
AC Botha	run out (Sammy)	**0**	3	7	0	0	0.00
GH Dockrell	b Benn	**19**	22	19	3	0	100.00
WB Rankin	not out	**5**	11	9	0	0	55.55
Extras	(lb 4, w 3, nb 1)	**8**					
Total	(all out; 49 overs; 217 mins)	**231**	(4.71 runs per over)				

Fall: 1-6 (Stirling, 1.4 ov), 2-42 (Porterfield, 11.6 ov), 3-86 (NJ O'Brien, 20.6 ov), 4-177 (Joyce, 37.3 ov), 5-187 (KJ O'Brien, 39.4 ov), 6-199 (Wilson, 41.4 ov), 7-199 (Cusack, 42.2 ov), 8-201 (Botha, 43.4 ov), 9-215 (Mooney, 45.5 ov), 10-231 (Dockrell, 48.6 ov)

	O	M	R	W	Econ	
KAJ Roach	8	0	34	1	4.25	
SJ Benn	10	0	53	4	5.30	(2w)
DJG Sammy	10	3	31	3	3.10	
AD Russell	10	2	37	1	3.70	(1nb)
KA Pollard	5	0	32	0	6.40	(1w)
NO Miller	6	0	40	0	6.66	

Toss: Ireland, who chose to field
Umpires: EAR de Silva (Sri Lanka) and SK Tarapore
Match referee: RS Mahanama (Sri Lanka)
West Indies won by 44 runs

Attendance: 9,537
TV umpire: BNJ Oxenford (Australia)
Reserve umpire: SJ Davis (Australia)
Player of the match: KA Pollard (West Indies)

SCORECARDS

SOUTH AFRICA V IRELAND
Eden Gardens, Kolkata   15 March 2011 - day/night

South Africa		R	M	B	4s	6s	SR
HM Amla	c Dockrell b Rankin	18	20	17	1	1	105.88
GC Smith*	run out (Mooney)	7	43	18	0	0	38.88
MN van Wyk†	b Dockrell	42	48	41	7	1	102.43
JH Kallis	run out (†N O'Brien/P'rfield)	19	43	31	3	0	61.29
JP Duminy	c **K O'Brien** b Mooney	99	139	103	6	1	96.11
F du Plessis	c Johnston b Stirling	11	21	19	0	0	57.89
CA Ingram	b Johnston	46	55	43	7	0	106.97
J Botha	not out	21	47	28	1	0	75.00
RJ Peterson	not out	0	1	0	0	0	-
Extras	(b 2, lb 3, w 4)	9					
Total	(7 wkts; 50 overs; 213 mins)	272	(5.44 runs per over)				

Did not bat M Morkel, DW Steyn

Fall : 1-24 (Amla, 4.4 ov), 2-52 (Smith, 9.4 ov), 3-84 (van Wyk, 15.5 ov), 4-95 (Kallis, 20.3 ov),5-117 (du Plessis, 26.3 ov), 6-204 (Ingram, 39.4 ov), 7-269 (Duminy, 49.4 ov)

	O	M	R	W	Econ	
WB Rankin	10	0	59	1	5.90	(1w)
DT Johnston	10	0	76	1	7.60	(1w)
JF Mooney	8	0	36	1	4.50	
GH Dockrell	10	0	37	1	3.70	
PR Stirling	10	0	45	1	4.50	(1w)
AR Cusack	2	0	14	0	7.00	(1w)

Ireland (target: 273 from 50 overs)		R	M	B	4s	6s	SR
WTS Porterfield*	c Smith b Morkel	6	8	8	1	0	75.00
PR Stirling	c Kallis b Morkel	10	15	11	2	0	90.90
EC Joyce	lbw b Botha	12	46	24	2	0	50.00
NJ O'Brien†	c †van Wyk b Kallis	10	23	16	0	1	62.50
GC Wilson	lbw b Peterson	31	60	48	4	1	64.58
KJ O'Brien	**c Amla b Peterson**	**19**	**39**	**24**	**2**	**0**	**79.16**
AR Cusack	c Smith b Peterson	7	23	11	1	0	63.63
JF Mooney	c †van Wyk b Kallis	14	49	28	1	0	50.00
DT Johnston	c †van Wyk b Duminy	12	14	16	0	1	75.00
GH Dockrell	c †van Wyk b Morkel	16	19	12	3	0	133.33
WB Rankin	not out	0	3	2	0	0	0.00
Extras	(w 4)	4					
Total	(all out; 33.2 overs; 154 mins)	141	(4.23 runs per over)				

Fall: 1-8 (Porterfield, 1.6 ov), 2-19 (Stirling, 3.3 ov), 3-35 (NJ O'Brien, 8.5 ov), 4-51 (Joyce, 11.5 ov),5-92 (KJ O'Brien, 21.3 ov), 6-92 (Wilson, 21.5 ov), 7-107 (Cusack, 25.5 ov), 8-123 (Johnston, 29.5 ov),9-137 (Mooney, 32.4 ov), 10-141 (Dockrell, 33.2 ov)

	O	M	R	W	Econ	
DW Steyn	4	1	13	0	3.25	
M Morkel	5.2	0	33	3	6.18	(2w)
JH Kallis	6	1	20	2	3.33	
J Botha	8	0	32	1	4.00	(1w)
RJ Peterson	8	0	32	3	4.00	
JP Duminy	2	0	11	1	5.50	

Toss: Ireland, who chose to field
Umpires: HDPK Dharmasena (Sri Lanka) & BR Doctrove (WI)
Match referee: RS Madugalle (Sri Lanka)
South Africa won by 131 runs

Attendance: 30,000
TV umpire: SJA Taufel (Australia)
Reserve umpire: IJ Gould (England)
Player of the match: JP Duminy (South Africa)

NETHERLANDS V IRELAND
Eden Gardens, Kolkata   18 March 2011

Netherlands		R	M	B	4s	6s	SR
ES Szwarczynski	c †N O'Brien b Johnston	1	8	4	0	0	25.00
W Barresi	lbw b Stirling	44	61	49	4	2	89.79
TLW Cooper	c Porterfield b Rankin	5	7	5	1	0	100.00
RN ten Doeschate	c Mooney b Stirling	106	166	108	13	1	98.14
AN Kervezee	c **K O'Brien** b Mooney	12	34	16	2	0	75.00
PW Borren*	c Porterfield b Mooney	84	108	82	10	0	102.43
AF Buurman†	run out (†N O'Brien)	26	49	30	4	0	86.66
Mudassar Bukhari	run out (Mooney/†N O'Brien)	11	22	8	0	1	137.50
PM Seelaar	run out (Mooney)	0	1	1	0	0	0.00
Adeel Raja	run out (Joyce/**K O'Brien**)	0	1	0	0	0	-
BP Loots	not out	0	1	0	0	0	-
Extras	(b 1, lb 8, w 5, nb 3)	17					
Total	(all out; 50 overs; 234 mins)	306	(6.12 runs per over)				

Fall: 0-7* (Barresi, ret not out, 1.3 ov), 1-7 (Szwarczynski, 1.3 ov), 2-12 (Cooper, 2.3 ov), 3-53 (Kervezee, 10.1 ov), 4-113 (Barresi, 21.5 ov), 5-234 (ten Doeschate, 39.5 ov), 6-287 (Borren, 46.5 ov), 7-305 (Buurman, 49.3 ov), 8-305 (Seelaar, 49.4 ov), 9-305 (Adeel Raja, 49.5 ov), 10-306 (Bukhari, 49.6 ov)

	O	M	R	W	Econ	
WB Rankin	9	0	74	1	8.22	(3nb, 3w)
DT Johnston	10	1	50	1	5.00	
JF Mooney	10	0	59	2	5.90	
GH Dockrell	3.4	0	15	0	4.09	
PR Stirling	10	0	51	2	5.10	
AR Cusack	2.2	0	15	0	6.42	
KJ O'Brien	**5**	**0**	**33**	**0**	**6.60**	**(2w)**

Ireland (target: 307 from 50 overs)		R	M	B	4s	6s	SR
WTS Porterfield*	c †Buurman b Cooper	68	116	93	10	0	73.11
PR Stirling	c Kervezee b Seelaar	101	119	72	14	2	140.27
EC Joyce	c †Buurman b Cooper	28	45	33	3	0	84.84
NJ O'Brien†	not out	57	83	58	7	0	98.27
GC Wilson	c †Buurman b ten Doeschate	27	26	21	2	2	128.57
KJ O'Brien	**not out**	**15**	**13**	**9**	**0**	**2**	**166.66**
Extras	(lb 10, w 1)	11					
Total	(4 wkts; 47.4 overs; 203 mins)	307	(6.44 runs per over)				

Did not bat: AR Cusack, DT Johnston, JF Mooney, GH Dockrell, WB Rankin

Fall: 1-177 (Porterfield, 26.6 ov), 2-179 (Stirling, 27.3 ov), 3-233 (Joyce, 38.1 ov), 4-279 (Wilson, 44.3 ov)

	O	M	R	W	Econ	
Mudassar Bukhari	7	0	42	0	6.00	
Adeel Raja	8	1	44	0	5.50	
BP Loots	2	0	29	0	14.50	
RN ten Doeschate	9	1	58	1	6.44	(1w)
PM Seelaar	9.4	1	55	1	5.68	
PW Borren	5	0	38	0	7.60	
TLW Cooper	7	1	31	2	4.42	

Toss: Ireland, who chose to field
Umpires: BR Doctrove (West Indies) and IJ Gould (England)
Match referee: RS Madugalle (Sri Lanka)
Ireland won by 6 wickets (with 14 balls remaining)

Attendance: 29,000
TV umpire: HDPK Dharmasena (Sri Lanka)
Reserve umpire: EAR de Silva (Sri Lanka)
Player of the match: PR Stirling (Ireland)

WORLD CUP AVERAGES

BATTING AVERAGES

	Mat	Inns	NO	Runs	HS	Ave	BF	SR	100	50	0	4s	6s
NJ O'Brien	6	6	1	205	57*	**41.00**	271	75.64	0	1	0	17	2
KJ O'Brien	**6**	**6**	**1**	**198**	**113**	**39.60**	**158**	**125.31**	**1**	**0**	**0**	**19**	**9**
GC Wilson	4	4	0	122	61	**30.50**	145	84.13	0	1	0	12	4
WTS Porterfield	6	6	0	180	75	**30.00**	270	66.66	0	2	1	21	1
EC Joyce	6	6	0	176	84	**29.33**	264	66.66	0	1	0	18	0
PR Stirling	6	6	0	157	101	**26.16**	128	122.65	1	0	1	23	3
AR Cusack	5	4	0	80	47	**20.00**	104	76.92	0	0	0	7	1
JF Mooney	6	5	1	58	33*	**14.50**	90	64.44	0	0	1	8	0
GH Dockrell	6	4	1	42	19	**14.00**	53	79.24	0	0	0	6	0
DT Johnston	5	4	1	42	17	**14.00**	46	91.30	0	0	0	4	1
AC Botha	2	2	0	22	22	**11.00**	43	51.16	0	0	1	2	0
WB Rankin	6	4	3	9	5*	**9.00**	25	36.00	0	0	0	0	0
AR White	2	2	0	15	10	**7.50**	37	40.54	0	0	0	1	0
A van der Merwe	0												
N Jones	0												

BOWLING AVERAGES

	Mat	Inns	Overs	Mdns	Runs	Wkts	BBI	Ave	Econ	SR	4wi
AC Botha	2	2	19.0	1	88	4	3/32	**22.00**	4.63	28.5	0
JF Mooney	6	6	45.0	0	259	10	4/63	**25.90**	5.75	27.0	1
KJ O'Brien	**6**	**4**	**17.0**	**0**	**115**	**4**	**4/71**	**28.75**	**6.76**	**25.5**	**1**
GH Dockrell	6	6	46.4	2	207	7	2/23	**29.57**	4.43	40.0	0
DT Johnston	5	5	43.2	2	240	8	2/16	**30.00**	5.53	32.5	0
PR Stirling	6	6	46.0	0	208	4	2/51	**52.00**	4.52	69.0	0
WB Rankin	6	6	55.0	2	315	3	1/35	**105.00**	5.72	110.0	0
AR White	2	1	5.0	0	23	0	-	-	4.60	-	0
AR Cusack	5	5	18.2	1	108	0	-	-	5.89	-	0

FIELDING STATS

4 catches	Porterfield
3 catches	N O'Brien (+ 1 stumping), **K O'Brien** Dockrell Johnston
2 catches	Stirling White Mooney
1 catch	Botha Rankin Cusack

POUCHED: *TJ snaps up Tim Bresnan in Bangalore*

STATISTICS

IRISH RECORDS (to end of World Cup)

Top ten run scorers

	Name	Mts	Inn	NO	50s	100s	HS	Avg	Runs
1	SJS Warke	114	151	10	28	4	144*	30.32	4275
2	WTS Portf'd	120	127	7	19	8	166	33.53	4023
3	AR White	189	167	28	16	5	152*	27.94	3884
4	IJ Anderson	86	141	25	13	7	198*	32.56	3777
5	K McCallan	226	196	41	11	2	100	23.33	3616
6	AC Botha	141	140	10	13	6	186	27.74	3606
7	DA Lewis	121	145	20	20	4	136*	28.63	3579
8	NJ O'Brien	114	119	19	19	6	176	35.29	3529
9	KJ O'Brien	143	139	25	16	4	171*	29.73	3389
10	AR Dunlop	114	128	20	16	4	150	29.30	3164

Top ten innings

	Name	Date	Opposition	Ground	Runs
1	EJG Morgan	10 Feb 2007	UAE	Sheikh Zayed Abu Dhabi	209*
2	IJ Anderson	14 Sep 1973	Canada	Toronto CC	198*
3	JP Bray	23 Oct 2005	UAE	Wanderers CC Windoek	190
4	AC Botha	9 Aug 2007	Scotland	Stormont	186
5	PR Stirling	7 Sep 2010	Canada	Toronto CC	177
6	NJ O'Brien	23 Oct 2005	UAE	Wanderers CC Windoek	176
7	NJ O'Brien	6 Mar 2008	UAE	Sheikh Zayed Abu Dhabi	174
8	AC Botha	9 Jul 2008	Netherlands	Hazelaarweg Rotterdam	172
9	KJ O'Brien	11 Oct 2008	Kenya	Gymkhana, Nairobi	171*
10	Sir TC O'Brien	26 May 1902	Oxford University	The Parks, Oxford	167

Top ten batting averages

	Name	Mts	Inn	NO	Runs	HS	Avg
1	MA Masood	40	55	5	1940	138	38.80
2	EJG Morgan	63	62	6	2075	209*	37.05
3	EC Joyce	57	58	7	1854	115*	36.35
4	TG McVeagh	21	36	5	1108	109	35.74
5	NJ O'Brien	114	119	19	3529	176	35.29
6	WTS Porterfield	120	127	7	4023	166	33.53
7	IJ Anderson	86	141	25	3777	198*	32.56
8	JP Bray	83	90	2	2812	190	31.95
9	SJS Warke	114	151	10	4275	144*	30.32
10	MP Rea	52	71	3	2044	115	30.06
(11)	KJ O'Brien	143	139	25	3389	171*	29.73

Top five strike rates

	Name	Mts	Inn	NO	Runs	Balls	S/Rate
1	DT Johnston	144	121	26	2155	2566	83.90
2	PR Stirling	76	81	2	2152	2711	79.38
3	KJ O'Brien	143	139	25	3389	4536	74.71
4	JF Mooney	106	87	24	1463	1861	74.69
5	AC Botha	141	140	10	3606	4327	72.08

Six sixes in an innings

	Name	Date	Opposition	Ground	Sixes
1	KJ O'Brien	11 Oct 2008	Kenya	Gymkhana, Nairobi	12
2	PJ Davy	5 Aug 1999	MCC	Lord's	8
3	G Dros	28 Aug 2003	Hertfordshire	Bishop's Stortford	7
4	AR Dunlop	21 Aug 1999	Scotland	Ormeau, Belfast	6
	JD Curry	30 Mar 1997	Singapore	Kuala Lumpur	6
	KJ O'Brien	2 Feb 2007	Kenya	Ruaraka, Nairobi	6
	KJ O'Brien	18 May 2009	Hampshire	Rose Bowl	6
	KJ O'Brien	2 Mar 2011	England	Chinnaswamy, Bangalore	6